No More Debt!

God's Strategy for Debt Cancellation

Other Books by Dr. Creflo A. Dollar Jr.

The Miracle of Debt Release
How to Get Out of Debt God's Way
Total Life Prosperity
The Anointing to Live
Lord, Teach Me How to Love
Understanding God's Purpose for the Anointing

Visit our Web site:
www.worldchangers.org

No More Debt!

God's Strategy for Debt Cancellation

Dr. Creflo A. Dollar Jr.

ISBN 1-885072-40-6
Copyright © 2000 Dr. Creflo A. Dollar Jr.

Published by:
Creflo Dollar Ministries
P.O. Box 490124
College Park, GA 30349

CONTENTS

Introduction

It's Time to Get Out of Debt!

Introduction

It's Time to Get Out of Debt!

"...And thou shalt be a blessing... and in thee shall all families of the earth be blessed" (Genesis 12:2,3).

Do you ever wonder how life would be without debt? I used to. For years my wife, Taffi, and I struggled to make ends meet. By the time we finished writing checks for school loans, car notes, rent, credit card bills, and monthly utilities, we barely had enough to survive until the next payday. With the addition of children, we discovered that our income was no match for our debt. It didn't take long for us to realize that we needed more than credit counseling or debt consolidation to get out of the fix we were in—we needed a miracle!

Perhaps you're in a similar situation. It seems like the harder you work, the more bills you pay; and the more bills you pay, the harder you have to work. But there is hope! You don't have to be trapped in debt for the rest of your life. There is an anointing available for debt release! By that I mean there is a special burden-removing, yoke-destroying power of God available to change your financial picture forever. In addition, there are also several Word-based principles that will, when applied consistently, release that anointing over your finances. I know this to be true because I've applied them to my own life with great success.

God Wants Us to Prosper

The first thing I had to realize, however, is that God wants His people to prosper. It grieved Him to see Taffi and me struggling to pay our monthly obligations. Psalm 35:27 says that He delights in the prosperity, or financial success, of His people. Many Christians find that hard to believe. In fact, they'd rather believe that poverty is a sign of holiness rather than the truth of God's Word.

What you must realize, however, is that debt is a demonic spirit designed to keep you from experiencing the abundant life that Jesus made available to us in John 10:10. It destroys marriages, damages credibility, and drives people to suicide, murder and bankruptcy. These cycles are not a part of God's plan of prosperity for His people. And it certainly isn't His will for your life. Why continue to settle for "not enough" when the Word says He wants to give you more than enough to meet your needs?

The Time Is Now

Now is the time to apply faith pressure on the anointing of debt release! As Christians living in these last days, it is vital that we get out and stay out of debt. Why? So we can fulfill the mandate given to Abraham in Genesis 12:3, to be blessed to be a blessing until all families of the earth are blessed. But you can't do that when you're living from paycheck to paycheck, struggling to make ends meet. You must get out of debt once and for all—not only for your sake, but also for the sake of those who have yet to experience God and the immeasurable benefits of living in His perfect will.

You see, God wants us to experience total life prosperity. This includes mental, physical, spiritual, and financial wholeness. For example, if you're sick and cannot afford medical treatment, you're living in lack instead of wholeness. But in order to walk in the abundance and total prosperity promised in God's Word, you must first stake your claim to it.

Matthew 11:12 tells us that "...*the kingdom of heaven suffereth violence, and the violent take it by force.*" In other words, prosperity will not fall out of the sky and into your lap. There are biblical principles that must be applied to your situations and circumstances before you see the manifestation of debt release. And the only way to apply those principles is to first destroy old patterns of thinking and develop a new mindset concerning debt and prosperity. A renewed mind is an important key to debt release. You cannot get out of debt if you believe that Christians are supposed to be poor. How can an impoverished people bring honor to a wealthy God Who owns everything? That's ridiculous!

Sadly, over 90% of the Body of Christ is in debt, without a clue as to how to get out and stay out of financial bondage. Part of the problem is that for too long, Christians have misread 1 Timothy 6:10, *"For the love of money is the root of all evil...."* Many interpret that scripture to mean that money is the root of all evil. Nothing could be farther from the truth! It's the *love of money*—having a wrong relationship with money—that is evil. Why? You can't fill a spiritual void with material things. That's called materialism.

God Has a Purpose

God's purpose for your debt deliverance is not so you can go and purchase designer clothes, fancy furniture, large homes, and expensive cars. Those things are by-products of prosperity, not the ultimate purpose for it. In Isaiah 55:8 God tells us, *"For my thoughts are not your thoughts, neither are your ways my ways...."* God never delivers you out of something just for your personal gain. Instead, your deliverance always benefits someone else. In other words, He has a plan for getting you out of debt and a purpose for putting money into your hands. It's not enough to just get out of debt and hoard the wealth. You must be ready to yield to God and allow Him to direct you in your spending and saving, and more importantly, in your giving. Why? Because whether you realize it or not, there are millions of people who have yet to hear the gospel, and your money can assist God in His mission to get the good news to the lost.

Every Christian has an obligation to get out

of debt. As the seed of Abraham (Galatians 3:29), God has given us an inheritance that must be used for the advancement of His kingdom. It's time to lay hold of all that is ours in the heavenly realm and manifest it here on earth. *The Amplified Bible* tells us in Romans 13:11, "*...you know what [a critical] hour this is, how it is high time now for you to wake up out of your sleep (rouse to reality). For salvation (final deliverance) is nearer to us now than when we first believed (adhered to, trusted in, and relied on Christ, the Messiah)."* Now the word *salvation* means more than just being born again. The Hebrew translation is *soteria,* meaning "deliverance, protection, soundness, prosperity, health, and preservation." In other words, your hour of deliverance is here!

God's Way Works!

During our first years of marriage, Taffi and I were up to our eyeballs in debt. We were making what they used to call "chump change" back then.

We lived in an apartment at the time, and I remember having to give my car a good push every once in a while to get it started. Yet in spite of our financial dilemma, God instructed me to teach the Word of God with simplicity and understanding to the Body of Christ throughout the world. But how could I do that? I could hardly make it from one payday to the next!

Finally, I threw up my hands in surrender and told God, "We can't live like this anymore! You've got to have a better plan. Show me!" And He did. Through the study of His Word and from some of the teachings of men I consider generals on this subject, our lives changed drastically. It began with a decision to get out of debt, a changed mindset, and positive, Word-based confessions. My heart's desire was to become a millionaire, so I began to say, "I'm a millionaire!" daily.

Today, that confession has become a reality. But it didn't happen overnight. And along the way I was ridiculed by many. However, consistency is the key to the breakthrough. Taffi and I have not only been delivered from debt, but we've also been delivered from people and what they say about us. In addition, we've been able to help others get out of debt. Believe me, Child of God, His way works!

If you are fed up with juggling bills, hiding from creditors and living from paycheck to paycheck, this book is for you! *No More Debt!* will give you the practical steps necessary to bring you out and keep you out of debt forever while ushering you into the abundant, prosperous life promised in God's Word.

The time is over for wondering if your dreams of living the "good life" will ever come true. It's time to begin seeing the manifestation of your prayers and live the life God intended for each of us. Child of God, it's time to get out of debt now!

1

A New Way
of Life

Chapter 1

A New Way of Life

"...But this one thing I do, forgetting those things which are behind, and reaching forth unto those things which are before, I press toward the mark for the prize of the high calling of God in Christ Jesus" (Philippians 3:13,14).

The way we live today is much different than years before. Almost everything in this world's system is based on the quick-fix method. Think of the advertisements you hear and see almost daily. For example, "Lose 30 pounds in 30 days," or "Consolidate your bills today." In this age of microwave ovens, supersonic travel and e-mail, it seems nearly impossible for us to wait patiently for things to happen—especially when it concerns our finances.

However, one thing is true: the process of getting in debt is certainly faster than the process for getting out. In fact, waiting to get the money to meet your monthly obligations takes much longer than pulling it out of your wallet to pay for something you want. Simply put, where you are now in your finances is the result of the choices you have made. "Brother Dollar, are you telling me that I'm in debt because I chose to be?" Well, yes! Whether you realize it or not, there are two systems at work in the financial realm— God's system and the world's system—and you have chosen to operate in the one that perpetuates debt.

Two Systems at Work

Throughout the New Testament, Jesus frequently spoke of the *kingdom of God.* What He referred to was one of two systems available for handling finances. When you break down the word *kingdom,* the prefix *king* refers to a person or figure, while the suffix *dom* refers to *dominion,* or sphere of influence. In other words, *kingdom* refers to an individual's realm of jurisdiction. The Kingdom of God then, is the manner in which God operates, or God's way of doing things. The same thing can be said of the words *world* and *worldly*—both refer to a method, or standard of operation. For example, when you say someone is "worldly," you're saying they are living according to what the world considers an acceptable standard of behavior. When you consider these definitions in the context of debt release, you are faced with a choice— either get out of debt God's way, or the world's way.

Most of us have already tried to get out of debt through the world's system of bill consolidation, second mortgages, credit counseling, or bankruptcy. However, none of these methods permanently resolve the problem because they foster dependency. Think about it. You borrow money only to have to borrow more to pay for the money you already owe. And on top of owing money to the lending company, you have to pay interest too! The same is true of financial promotion.

For example, if you purchase an item with your credit card and make the monthly payment on time, every time—guess what? Your credit limit increases. The more you buy, the more you're able to buy. But, again you have to pay interest, which means that you're actually paying more for the item than you originally would have if you had simply waited to buy it with cash! It just doesn't make sense. Whether you want to admit it or not, the world's system promotes debt. In addition, it teaches you to put away money while you're young so that you can become wealthy when you are old. Although that sounds reasonable, and I certainly believe in saving money, I think most of us would prefer to be millionaires at 30, 40, 50, and 60. Child of God, no matter how you look at it, the world's system is just another trick of the enemy to keep you in bondage.

The Bible refers to Satan as the ruler of this present world (John 12:31;16:11). Therefore, the world's system, or way of doing things, belongs to him.

On the other hand, God's system promotes prosperity, peace and the gospel message. Jesus said, "...*My kingdom is not of this world...*" (John 18:36). In other words, God's system goes completely against the status quo.

The Better Way

The way God's system works is through something called seedtime and harvest. Let me explain. Do you remember the golden rule: "Do unto others as you would have them do unto you?" This statement actually refers to the principle of sowing and reaping found in Galatians 6:7, "*...for whatsoever a man soweth, that shall he also reap....*" Simply put, whatever you do to or for others will come back to you, whether it's good or bad.

This same rule can also be applied to finances. Continuous overspending leads to debt accumulation. Running up charges on your credit card by recklessly buying any and everything you want will only lead to a harvest of insufficiency. But, by becoming a good steward over your money, you promote increase and abundance in your life.

Realistically, your best choice is to turn to the Word of God for the solution to your debt problem. Second Samuel 22:31 says, *"As for God, his way is perfect; the word of the Lord is tried...."* In other words, the Word of God works! But it's up to us to apply those principles to our situations and circumstances.

However, most of us have taken God's way of doing things and combined them with the ways of the world. And we think it's all right to do that! Jesus said in Revelation 3:15,16, *"...I would thou wert cold or hot. So then because thou art lukewarm, and neither cold nor hot, I will spue thee out of my mouth."* You can't expect to get out of debt by trying to blend God's way of seedtime and harvest with the world's system. For example, don't decide to file bankruptcy this week and then begin following God's plan next week. That would be the same as trying to get saved through your own good deeds. It just doesn't work.

So what do you do? Make a quality decision to

divorce yourself from the world's system, and instead begin to employ God's method of sowing and reaping. God has a perfect plan to get you out of debt, but if you continue to run back to your former way of doing things, you'll never get anywhere. *The Amplified Bible* version of Matthew 6:33 commands us to *"...seek (aim at and strive after) first of all His kingdom and His righteousness (His way of doing and being right)..."* so that God may grant us the things we desire. In others words, when you do things God's way, you make it easy for Him to move on your behalf. Believe me, this plan works!

Sow a Seed, Reap a Harvest

God's system is based on giving and receiving. Sounds like a strange way to get out of debt, doesn't it? Let me explain. God's system is the exact opposite of the world's system. The world tells you to hoard every penny you've got, while God tells you to give in order to get out of debt. The key is obedience to God in your giving.

If you desire to get out of debt, it's absolutely vital that you learn to give under the direction of the Holy Spirit. In Luke 6:38, Jesus says to "give" so that *"...it shall be given unto you; good measure, pressed down, and shaken together, and running over, shall men give into your bosom...."* Take a look at the first part of this verse. *"Give, and it shall be given unto you...."* Giving to others causes others to give to you. And whatever you give will be returned to you.

It's important to understand that the way out of debt is not through your paycheck. Why? Because your job won't pay enough to take care of you and everything God has told you to do. Your job is just an avenue by which you can collect seed to sow into the lives of those around you. Consider the call of God on my life. I could make millions of dollars a year, and it still would not be enough to pay for the television programming needed to reach the millions of people who have yet to hear the gospel for the first time or who need to be discipled on a daily basis.

The way out of debt is through giving. Give to live, and then live to give. Take a look at Matthew 13:3.

I call this the grandfather parable of them all, because if you can get a good understanding of this, you will probably understand just about everything else in the Bible. It says, "...*Behold, a sower went forth to sow....*" Now stop right there. A farmer has to sow if he wants a harvest. And just as he will never harvest a crop by hoarding his seed, neither will you get out of debt by hoarding your money.

It's vital that you begin to see money as a means to an end. Money is just a tool that God can use to further the gospel. You work in order to get seed to plant into good ground. In the same way that a farmer lives off of the harvest of his crop, so you too should live on the harvest of the seed you have sown. However, a farmer needs seed before he can make a living.

This mindset is a problem for many Christians. They think it's okay to give every now and again, but to give all of the time...no way! It's one thing to say, "I want to be out of debt," but it's something entirely different to become disciplined enough to actually get there. You see, the way in which you handle your finances pretty much determines how you handle everything else in life. Just take a look at your checkbook. How many entries are penned to God? How many entries are for your own needs and desires?

Learn to Give

Learning to give is fundamental to Christianity. Your willingness to give to others is the measuring stick of your spiritual maturity. That's a tough pill to swallow, considering that most Christians treat giving as a grievous obligation rather than a joy. In 2 Corinthians 9:7, Paul states that *"...God loveth a cheerful giver."* In other words, there is no real benefit in reluctant giving. It makes God feel as if you really don't want anything to do with His plans and purposes. And believe it or not, when you give grudgingly, that is exactly what you are doing—resenting God's ultimate plan of funding the message of the gospel. Not only that, but reluctant feelings lead to a sense of loss. Sowing seed should not be seen as loss, but as gain. You're releasing something in order to get a hundred-fold return on what you have sown. And there are few investments, if any, that yield a hundred-fold return.

Once you begin the process of sowing, make it a way of life. Don't sow to clear your conscience, because it won't work. I have people in my congregation who put money on the altar out of obedience to God, and then I have people who do it without hearing from Him or expecting anything in return. That's wrong! The right action with the wrong motive won't get you very far. *Always* give with the expectation of reaping a hundred-fold from what you have sown!

Now before you sow, you should remember to:

1. Renew your mind.

Without renewing your mind, you won't be able to give. You'll still be thinking that you are losing something instead of gaining something. It's important to get the Word on the subject of giving. Without it, you're not sowing; instead, you're just giving money away. What's the difference? The difference is that when you sow, you know beyond a shadow of a doubt that your seed will bring a hundred-fold return. Give without fear! The Word of God assures you in Luke 8:5-8 that abundance is on the way when you sow into the right ground.

2. Sow into good ground.

You shouldn't sow your seed just any place. Some examples of good ground include certain ministries, special projects, the lives of other believers, and the life of your man or woman of God. You will only receive a harvest from the seed sown into good ground. And remember to sow only where God tells you to sow. He's the only One who knows what is inside a person's heart. In 1 Samuel 16:7, He told the prophet Samuel *"...the Lord seeth not as man seeth; for man looketh on the outward appearance, but the Lord looketh on the heart."* Don't be deceived by outward appearances. Trust God for direction and allow Him to guide your giving. You'll receive a tremendous harvest when you obey.

3. Give expecting to receive.

This may sound selfish, but it's a biblical principle. Jesus stated in Luke 6:38 that when you give, it will be given back to you. For example, the human body can only exhale for a certain amount of time before it signals a need for oxygen. At that point, the body inhales, rejuvenating the system. It's a cycle instituted by God: inhale, exhale, inhale, exhale. We will die if we do only one or the other. The same is true in the area of giving and receiving. You can't just give all of the time. Receiving is the other half of the cycle. If you don't receive, you won't have what you need or any seed left to give to others.

4. Remember that a seed grows down before it grows up.

The Bible tells us in Mark 4:26,27 that the Kingdom of God is *"...as if a man should cast seed into the ground; And should sleep, and rise night and day, and the seed should spring and grow up, he knoweth not how."* In other words, allow some time for your seed to grow and develop. Don't put it in the ground and then stand over it. Your harvest will come only after the root has grown deep into the ground of your heart. By planting the Word of God in your heart, saying your faith scriptures aloud several times a day and acting on your faith, you will see results in no time.

5. Help others with a similar need.

If you want God to release you from your debt, sow the seed of debt release into someone else's life. The same force you exert to help someone out of their debt opens the door for God to get you out of debt. The Word of God says in Luke 6:38 *"...For with the same measure that ye mete withal it shall be measured unto you again."* In other words, what you want done for yourself, do for someone else first. If you want to buy a car debt free, contribute toward someone else's efforts to buy a car debt free. If you want your IRS loan cancelled, help someone who has to pay off an IRS loan.

You're probably thinking, "Brother Dollar, if I could do that, my debt would be paid off by now." I'm not asking you to pay off their debt. I am, however, encouraging you to give what God tells you to give in each circumstance. In better terms, start an out of debt flow. Activate your debt release by sowing continuously into the lives of others. It will move the hand of God.

✗ ✗ ✗ ✗

Begin today to apply the above-mentioned principles in your life. Turn away from the world's system of debt release, and cleave to God's method of seedtime and harvest. You are guaranteed to reap a hundred-fold return every time!

2
Tuning In
to God's Frequency

Chapter 2

Tuning In to God's Frequency

"And thine ears shall hear a word behind thee, saying, This is the way, walk ye in it, when ye turn to the right hand, and when ye turn to the left" (Isaiah 30:21).

Knowing how to hear the voice of God clearly and accurately is one of the most important things a Christian needs to learn. Why? Because God's voice provides the guidance and wisdom you and I need to get us from where we are now to where we want to be. It also eliminates any confusion as to what voice we are hearing—God's, the devil's or our own. Our inability or unwillingness to hear and recognize the voice of God prevents us from taking advantage of every spiritual and earthly blessing found in His Word. Simply put, we often miss our opportunity to be blessed because we are not spiritually in tune to God's frequency. It only takes one word from God to change our lives forever, but we must listen for that word.

Jesus told us in John 10:27, "*My sheep hear my voice, and I know them, and they follow me....*" As a child of God, it should be natural to recognize the voice of the Shepherd. If you don't know who's speaking to you, you will follow any voice you hear, and you'll open yourself up to all kinds of deceiving spirits. The bottom line is, you can either hear from God or from the devil, but only one voice will lead you to the solution to your problem.

A Hearing Heart Is Essential

True, continued success comes from hearing God's voice. That's how you can lay hold of the abundant life Jesus promised in John 10:10. And it's not enough to live on what you've heard in the past. God speaks daily, which means you must hear from Him daily if you want to be successful in life. Solomon, the wisest man who ever lived, knew this to be true. He was just a boy when King David died, and he knew absolutely nothing about ruling the kingdom. Yet he inherited the throne and became king. Solomon was wise enough to know that he lacked knowledge and experience in this area, so he turned to God for guidance and direction.

1 Kings 3:3-9

And Solomon loved the Lord...and [he] went to Gibeon to sacifice there; for that was the great high place: a thousand burnt offerings did Solomon offer upon that altar. In Gibeon the Lord appeared to Solomon in a dream by night: and God said, Ask what I shall give thee. And Solomon said...now, O Lord my God, thou hast made thy servant king instead of David my father: and I am but a little child: I know not how to go out or come in...Give therefore thy servant an understanding heart to judge thy people, that I may discern between good and bad: for who is able to judge this thy so great a people?

Notice what Solomon asked for—an understanding, or *hearing* heart. More than anything else, he wanted to be able to hear God clearly so he could rule God's people just as David did. God was so pleased with the request that He told Solomon, *"...Because thou hast asked this thing, and has not asked for thyself long life; neither hast asked riches for thyself...but has asked for thyself understanding to discern judgment; Behold, I have done according to thy words: lo, I have given thee a wise and an understanding heart... And I have also given thee...both riches, and honour..."* (vv. 11-13). God gave Solomon much more than he asked because he asked for the right thing—a hearing heart.

Most of us have the impression that we should ask for material wealth rather than wisdom. Solomon knew the opposite to be true. He asked for nothing more than to hear God speak clearly to him, and God blessed him with an abundance of wealth. His success was not based on the money he received but on his ability to hear from the One who gave him the wealth to begin with. That should be true of every

Christian. Jesus said in Matthew 6:33 that we are to seek first the kingdom of God (God's way of doing things), and then everything else—whatever you need or desire—will be added. Part of that everything is wealth. When you seek God, you are really seeking wisdom. And wisdom will lead you out of even the worst financial circumstance.

Now, the problem for most of us is not the fact that we can't hear God, but that we aren't really listening to Him. God is a great conversationalist. And He will speak to you at any time, whether you're driving, sitting still, or in the presence of others. He'll tell you things that will bless your socks off, if you will just listen. Hearing His voice requires that you keep silent and open your ears. Often when Christians pray, they do all the talking. A monologue is *not* a conversation. You can't be the one always talking and never listening. Try that on some of your friends and see what happens. Their eyes will glaze over, and they won't hear a thing you say. That may sound cruel, but the fact is, it's difficult to communicate with someone who talks so much that no one else can get a word in edgewise.

Neglect is another problem. You can't have a hit-and-miss relationship with God, and then expect Him to jump into action when you need help. Galatians 6:7 tells us that God cannot be mocked. You can't take advantage of God and then expect Him to move immediately on your behalf when the enemy comes in to steal, kill and destroy. That's selfish! It takes consistent effort from reading the Word and spending personal time with God daily to become close enough to recognize when He is speaking to you.

Get A Clear Signal

It's just like listening to the radio. What do you do when you want to hear a particular station or type of music? More than likely you hit a button that takes you to the station you want to hear. The key is in knowing what to listen for. If the wrong type of music comes up, you know you have the wrong station. That's the way it is with God. If you hear something that does not line up with His Word, it's not His voice. His voice is like a signal, and we tune our ears to His frequency. The signal remains constant day after day. He doesn't change His frequency or location, and He always "plays" what we need to hear.

Never think that God can't or won't speak directly to you. He will, if you spend time with Him and expect to hear from Him. Do you think a radio station has gone out of business just because you can't hear it from the other side of town? No! This same principle applies with God. Just because *you* can't hear Him, doesn't mean He's stopped talking. It just means that you aren't tuned in to His frequency.

Communing with God is never a waste of time. In fact, it's just the opposite. It's the best use of your time because it enables you to tap into greater levels of anointing, power, and revelation knowledge—things you need every day but are costly to obtain.

Now before I show you how to develop better hearing, let me explain a few of the things that can hinder you from hearing God's voice.

1. Unbelief.

How can God speak to you if you don't believe He will? I've met people who were shocked to hear me say, *"Here's what God told me this morning...."* They looked at me as if I'd lost my mind! The truth is, God desires to share things with you just as He did with Abraham, Moses, David, Solomon, and other great men and women of God.

Paul warned us in Hebrews 3:12 not to have *"...an evil heart of unbelief...."* By diligently studying the Word of God, we discover for ourselves what God has to say about the issues that concern us. It's impossible to have enough faith to believe for something unless you get in the Word and find out what God has to say about it. The Bible is a book of promises from a loving God to His children. If you can find it in there—whatever it is—He wants you to have it. And that includes debt release! It's up to you to decide whether you'll continue to entertain doubt and disbelief, or cast down those imaginations (2 Corinthians 10:5) and believe God for the best.

2. An undeveloped spirit.

An undeveloped spirit is a spirit with potential for growth, but one that lacks the motivation and desire to achieve it. Now, judge yourself honestly. Are you constantly maturing? Or are you on the same level of spirituality you were last year? Chances are, if you're not maturing, you're stagnating—and that's no place for a child of God to be.

At some point in time, children have to learn how to communicate with those around them. They can't gurgle and coo all of their lives. The same thing is true with God's people. We can't continue to be spoon-fed basic Bible doctrine forever. There comes a time in the life of every Christian when they must dig deeper into the Word in order to discover greater revelation to strengthen their faith. How do you do that? By constantly surrounding yourself with the people and resources that will help you in your quest for a deeper relationship with God.

Just as it's impossible for a child to learn English without first being constantly exposed to it, so too, is it impossible for a Christian to mature without being

47

exposed to the deeper truths of the gospel. You must learn how to "speak" God's language in order for you to mature and receive all that He has for you. Your spirit only grows through the studying of the Word, worship, and prayer. The Word builds up your faith, and an increase in faith will propel you to greater levels in God.

3. A hardened heart.

Hard soil is difficult to plow and impossible to sow seed in. That's exactly how God perceives you when you refuse to let go of past hurts. You're deceived if you think you can hold grudges and still expect God to move on your behalf. That's not how it works.

In Matthew 6:12 Jesus prayed, "And forgive us our debts, as we forgive our debtors." Notice that this is conditional. God forgives our debts—whether physical, financial, spiritual, mental, or emotional—when we first forgive those who we feel owe us something. "But Brother Dollar, you don't know what they did to me!" Child of God, it really doesn't matter when your miracle is on the line. "Well, I'll forgive, but I won't ever forget!" That's the wrong attitude to take. Unforgiveness opens the door for tormenting spirits such as low self-esteem, oppression and rejection to come into your life. They feed off of the negativity you harbor in your heart and shut out the voice of God. Why on earth would you hold on to something that's going to stop you from hearing a Word from God that could change your life?

Lay aside anything that hinders you from hearing God's voice so you can receive the miracle you're believing Him for. Make a quality decision to extend the same mercy and forgiveness to others that God extends to you. It's not easy to let go of past hurts, but the end result is worth it.

4. Take time to hear Him.

The word *blessed* means "empowered to prosper and excel." The ability to hear from God does just that. In Matthew 16:13, Jesus asked his disciples who they thought He was. Peter was the only one who received revelation knowledge from God to answer Him correctly. He said, *"...Thou art the Christ, the Son of the living God."* Jesus answered and said, *"...Blessed art thou, Simon Bar-jona: for flesh and blood hath not revealed it unto thee, but my Father which is in heaven. And I say also unto thee, That thou art Peter, and upon this rock I will build my church; and the gates of hell shall not prevail against it"* (Matthew 16:16-18). In other words, Jesus gave Peter the ability to succeed in anything he put his hand to. Why? Because he did not just shout out answers like the rest of the disciples; instead, he paused to receive new revelation from God.

How many times do we go through our day making decisions instead of allowing God to tell us what He would like us to do in each situation? How often do we make decisions based on emotion rather than wisdom, and then hope that He will bless it? The difference between an extraordinary and an average Christian lies in their ability to stop in the middle of a storm and hear clearly from God. What kind of a Christian are you? And what kind do you aspire to be?

Hearing from God builds your faith and confidence and enables you to endure hard times. You are able to hold on no matter what it looks like, feels like, or seems like. You have the assurance that God will make a way out of your circumstance or situation.

Abraham had this type of confidence. Paul tells us in Hebrews 11:17-19 that Abraham, out of obedience to God, willingly offered his only son, Isaac, as a sacrifice. He believed that God would raise Isaac from the dead because God had promised that a great nation would come from his seed (Genesis 12:2).

Here are five things you must do in order to position yourself to hear God's voice.

1. Maintain a spirit of expectancy.

God cannot say anything to you if you don't think He will talk to you. You speak to your spouse and to your children every day, and you expect them to talk to you every day as well. It's only when you are mad at each other that you go around the house without speaking. God is waiting for you to open yourself up

51

to hear from Him. In the same way that He wanted to commune with Adam and Eve in the Garden, He desires to speak to you.

Hebrews 13:8 tells us that Jesus Christ is the same yesterday, today, and forever. If that's the case, and the Word of God does not lie, then God desires to spend time with you daily. He is waiting for you to position yourself to hear His voice. Get rid of any doubt or religious thinking that tells you God no longer speaks to His people. That's ridiculous. He never changes. And if you give Him a chance, He'll prove it to you.

2. Pray in the Spirit without ceasing.

This will probably be difficult for people who don't believe in speaking in tongues. Romans 8:26 tells us that the Holy Spirit prays for and through us with words we cannot understand. Just because your natural mind can't understand your prayers in other tongues doesn't mean they aren't effective. They are! And they're more powerful than a prayer spoken in our natural tongue, because the Holy Spirit knows exactly what to pray for at all times. First Thessalonians 5:19 commands us not to put out the Spirit's fire. Don't grieve Him by denying Him the use of your vocal cords. In doing so, you could be denying yourself the manifestation of all you've been seeking God for.

Paul commanded us in 1 Thessalonians 5:17 to pray without ceasing. Now examine yourself. How many times do you pray a day? Is it just a token prayer at mealtime or in a barely audible voice first thing in the morning when you're only half awake? Or do you thank Him and acknowledge His presence all day long? Pray without ceasing means just that—without stopping. Just because your early morning prayer time is over doesn't mean that you can't talk to God while driving to and from work or while walking up and down the halls of your school or job. Practicing His presence is vital if you desire to hear His voice.

3. Confirm what you hear with the Word and wait for His peace.

Not every voice you hear will be from God—just

as not every phone call you receive during the day is the one you were expecting. Hearing from God should not be a deeply spiritual issue. I've met people who claimed to have received a "word from the Lord," and have gotten in trouble because of it. John tells us in 1 John 4:1 not to believe everything we hear, but to test the spirits speaking to us. Satan can appear as an angel of light (2 Corinthians 11:14) and will do anything he can to get you out of the will of God—including feeding you false information. God's instructions will always do the following:

- Line up with the written Word.
- Require faith and courage.
- Go against the "wisdom" of the world.
- Give you peace in your heart.

If what you have heard does not line up with these safeguards, chances are you did not hear from God at all. Remember, the devil will use every opportunity to deceive you if he thinks he can. Wait for the peace of God to confirm what you've heard. If you have any "funny feelings," it's the Holy Spirit letting you know that what you heard was not the voice of God.

4. Seek Godly counsel.

Proverbs 13:20 tells us that he who walks with the wise becomes wise. Sometimes we allow our own emotions to blind us to warning signs that may be present in our situations. The only remedy for that is to seek the counsel of mature believers who have proven themselves to be mature by the fruit they bear. Do not seek the counsel of an immature believer or an unsaved person, because neither has sufficient experience in dealing with the things of God. Seek counsel from those who can confirm God's voice to you through the Word of God.

5. Boldly obey God's instruction.

There's no point in hearing from God if you don't obey what He instructs you to do. Many times God tells us things in order to take us from one level of faith and anointing to the next. But you'll never get to where He wants you to be unless you surrender your will to

His. That's what the Bible calls true humility—complete and total submission to God's will. The bold, obedient Christian says, "I have heard God's voice. I am obeying, and nothing will move me." Hebrews 11:6 tells us that God rewards those who earnestly seek after Him. He desires those who boldly step out in faith and hold on at all costs. And without faith, it is impossible to please Him. I don't know about you, but I want to please God. And it's only those who please God that receive the manifestation of God's blessings.

✗   ✗   ✗   ✗

Hearing from God is a privilege that has been made available to us through the shed blood of Jesus. We no longer have to go through a variety of priests or be ceremonially cleansed before entering into communion with the Almighty. God desires that we position ourselves to hear His voice so we can receive the Word that will change our lives forever. It's only by seeking His face and entrusting ourselves to Him that we receive the ability to prosper and excel.

3
The Practical Side to Debt Cancellation

Chapter 3

The Practical Side to Debt Cancellation

"…Write the vision, and make it plain upon tables, that he may run that readeth it. For the vision is yet for an appointed time, but at the end it shall speak, and not lie: though it tarry, wait for it; because it will surely come, it will not tarry" (Habakkuk 2:2,3).

Getting out of debt involves much more than just wishing or hoping for it to happen. Instead, it involves hard work—both in the spiritual and the natural realm. It is a process whereby both you and God have vital parts to play. After all, it's not fair to expect Him to do His part (cancel the debt) without you first doing yours (planting the seed).

Sadly, many Christians mistakenly believe that getting out of debt is unrealistic. Others believe that while it may be possible for some, it is impossible for them. Let me clear up those misguided thoughts right now. The Word of God says that what God will do for one person, He will do for another. Romans 2:11 tells us that *"...there is no respect of persons with God."* And since Jesus is the same yesterday, today, and forever (Hebrews 13:8), we must accept the fact that they are both willing to do for us whatever they have committed themselves to do in the Word.

Destined for Prosperity

According to the inheritance package listed for us in Deuteronomy Chapter 28, God promises to *bless*, or "empower to prosper" our baskets and store (v.5). If we were to translate that into today's language, *baskets* would be our purses or wallets, and *store* would be our bank accounts, or the places we store money. Verse 8 tells us that the Lord will command His blessings on us. In verse 11, He promises to make us plenteous in goods. And finally verse 12 states that God wants to give to us His *"...good treasure...."* If you continue reading, you'll discover that the scripture says as His children we should *"...lend unto many... and...not borrow."*

However, Deuteronomy is not the only place in the Bible that talks about prosperity. Psalm 35:27 informs us that the Lord takes pleasure in the prosperity of those who serve Him. And in Psalm 115:14, David let us know that we should expect to increase more and more. Now I don't know about you, but if God wants to do all of that for me, I want to receive it! Still, you may be thinking, "Brother Dollar, that's the Old Testament! What does the New Testament have to say? Third John 2 sums it all up for us. *"Beloved, I wish above all things that thou mayest prosper and be in health, even as thy soul prospereth."* You see, it is the will of God that we live a prosperous life. But no one can do that if they are broke.

When I learned of the awesome promises God established just for me in His covenant with Abraham, it ended the debate in my mind—and it should do the same for you, too. You see, although God made this covenant with Abraham, we are Abraham's seed, or offspring. *"And if ye be Christ's, then ye are Abraham's seed, and heirs according to the promise"* (Galatians 3:29). Therefore, as born-again Christians, we have a covenant right to live prosperously and be free from debt.

So, the next time someone challenges you about prosperity and the "unrealistic" goal of becoming debt free, show them God's Word! There's enough ammunition in there to blow them out of the water. Don't let your family, friends, the devil, or even your own mind challenge what the Word of God says concerning this issue.

Now, if God can supernaturally cancel my debt and show me how to live debt-free forever, you must believe me when I tell you that He will do the same for you! It all begins with a quality decision to become debt free. And no matter what your financial picture may look like today, always keep Luke 1:37 in mind. *"For with God nothing shall be impossible."* However, you must first understand that God's strategy for debt cancellation will only work for those who trust Him. You must demonstrate your confidence in God at all times. How? By speaking the end from the beginning, just as He does. For example, you may be in debt today, but that doesn't mean you have to be in the same place tomorrow. Through Jesus Christ, the Anointed One and His Anointing, all things are possible! And not only are all things possible for Him, but according to Matthew 17:20, if you demonstrate a little bit of faith—the size of a mustard seed—nothing shall be impossible for *you*!

Get Yourself in Order

Now let's discuss the practical aspects of God's plan. Have you ever heard the phrase, "God can't bless your mess?" Well, that's actually true. You see, God is a God of order and discipline. He likes things organized and easily accessible. For example, He gave explicit instructions to Moses concerning the Tent of Meeting. All throughout Exodus, Leviticus, Numbers, and Deuteronomy, God told Moses who was to serve before Him, what they were to do and wear, when sacrifices were to be offered, and where the sacrifices were to be made. This prevented the Israelites from disrespecting the presence of God and serving Him in a haphazard way.

The same thing is true with your finances. God wants to help you get out of debt, but it's vitally important that you do your part and bring some order to your financial picture. Have you ever been in a room that was so messy, you had to spend time thinking about where to place your feet before trying to wade through the piles of dirty clothes, books, and garbage? That's the way God sees your finances when you don't know how much you owe your creditors. You are able to see the whole picture much better when everything is written down and drawn out. Simply organizing your bills and filing system will enable you to put a demand on the anointing to get you out of debt.

Here is a practical plan of action to help you get

out and stay out of debt. Applying these steps in your life requires discipline, determination, and diligence; however, the end results are worth it.

1. Renew your mind concerning debt release by the Word of God.

There are two reasons why renewing your mind is vital for debt release. First, you must understand that God wants you out of debt. It is your right as a Child of God. After all, you belong to the One Who owns the cattle on a thousand hills (Psalm 50:10). Why stay in bondage to creditors and this world's system when you have been given a covenant right to live free of debt and insufficiency?

Sadly, that's the way many believers would rather live their lives—trapped by debt and unable to help others as often as God directs them to. They piously say, "Oh, as long as I've got King Jesus...!" But that's the wrong attitude to take. We must desire to be out of debt because that's what *God* desires. Paul commanded us in Romans 13:8 to owe no man anything but love. It's important that you see debt-free living as an obtainable, desirable, God-given right. Otherwise you'll remain in the same predicament for the rest of your life.

Second, renewing the mind gets rid of the poverty mentality. A poverty mentality is one that is bound up by fear and suspicion. It sees giving as a loss rather than a gain. This is true of *religious* Christians. They give only so much before they become uncomfortable and afraid of not having enough. They don't understand that when God directs us to give, He is trying to get more *to* us, not take away the little we have. Test yourself. What was the last thing God instructed you to do financially? Did you give what He told you to give? If so, great! If not, you need to renew your mind in that area.

So how do you renew your mind? By diligently studying the Word of God concerning debt cancellation. This involves digging deep into the Scriptures to find every place where it mentions supernatural debt release. Looking up key words in the concordance is a good place to start. I also recommend these accounts concerning debt cancellation: the Israelite exodus from Egypt (Exodus 3:21,22;14:30,31), the man with the borrowed axe head (2 Kings 6:5,6) and the woman with the cruse of oil (1 Kings 17:10-16). By studying the miraculous, debt-canceling events mentioned in the Bible, your faith and confidence levels increase, enabling you to believe for your own debt cancellation. You will no longer say, "I know God can cancel debt, but will He do it for me?" Instead you will boldly declare, "God *will* cancel my debt, because He is no respecter of persons, but of faith."

God will cancel your debt if you give Him a chance to do so. But it's only when you have renewed your mind to the point where you are operating by faith, rather than fear that He is free to move in your finances. You must first understand the purpose for wealth defined in Genesis 12:2,3 before God will allow any of it to come into your hands. *"And I will make of thee a great nation, and I will bless thee, and make thy name great; and thou shalt be a blessing: And I will bless them that bless thee, and curse him that curseth thee: and in thee shall all families of the earth be blessed."* In clearer terms, God wants to bless you so that you can bless others throughout the earth. Deuteronomy 8:18 tells us that God wants us to be wealthy and out of debt in order to *"...establish his covenant...."* Begin now to see yourself out of debt! Develop a mental picture of prosperous living.

Once you have a solid understanding that the primary focus of money is to spread the gospel, you must get yourself ready for the overflow. That means wealthy living. Look through magazines and books for ideas on houses, land, clothes, and automobiles. Make a scrapbook of the things your heart desires most. Then make every effort to put the Word of God before your eyes, in your ears, and on your tongue.

You see, you must be spiritually wealthy before you can become materially wealthy. A proper understanding of money reduces the chances of you abusing it in the future. Your primary goal, once the money begins to manifest, should be to pay off your debt, and then whatever else God tells you to do with it. If He wants you to sow it into someone's life, do it! Remember, He's trying to get more money into your hands, and your obedience will open the door for that to happen. *"Give, and it shall be given unto you; good measure, pressed down, shaken together, and running over, shall men give into your bosom. For with the same measure that ye mete withal it shall be measured to you again" (Luke 6:38).*

Once God is confident that He can trust you with His money, His blessings will begin to overflow in your life. That's when your scrapbook will come in handy—you'll experience the joy of wealthy living here on earth!

2. Gather your bills into one place.

This is simple enough. Just gather all of your bills and put them in an easily accessible location. This can be a bag, desk drawer, accordion file, or manila folder. You may also wish to put cancelled checks and payment stubs in with your bills, for a quick and easy reference. Remember, order is a prerequisite for miracles to take place in your finances.

When you have accomplished this task, take a

sheet of paper and write on it the date and your declaration of independence from debt. It may say something like, "I'm out of debt, my needs are met, and I have plenty more to put in store!" Seeing these words and reading them aloud every time you go to pay a bill will bring in your harvest of debt cancellation. It may sound strange, but it will work.

When Taffi and I began this process, we immediately experienced demonic attacks. Nevertheless, we used that piece of paper as a point of contact for God's anointing to work on our behalf. Each time we prayed, we placed our hands on our bag of bills bearing the words "debt free" and made our confessions based on God's Word. Under the words "debt free" we wrote the things we were expecting to help us out of our situation: favor, unexpected income and debt-releasing anointing.

Each day, several times a day, we made our confessions, and soon our prayers for miraculous debt cancellation were answered. It took time, but the point is we no longer live the way we did then. Today, God is using us mightily to fulfill His covenant.

3. Create a list of every bill you owe and ask God for the specific financial miracle you need.

Knowing exactly how much you owe is vital. Why? What if someone was willing to pay off your credit card debt today? Could you tell them exactly how much you owe? If not, you could miss the favor presented to you by God. You see, God operates through people in order to cancel debts. But in order for Him to be able to do that, you must know how much debt you're in so that you can speak to that mountain and command it to be removed (Matthew 17:20). You do this by writing down the name of each creditor and the exact balance owed them. Then recite aloud the information you have written down. Confess what the Word has to say concerning debt cancellation and expect God to cancel every one, right down to the penny.

In addition, you may also find it helpful to draw a chart of how much you owe on a poster so that you can track your progress. Along the same lines, write that information in a notebook or on a piece of paper and put it in several places, such as your refrigerator, wallet, mirror, or computer. In this way, debt cancellation is in the forefront of your mind. Learn to speak to the mountain of debt in your life daily. By allowing the Word of God to come out of your mouth, you are applying faith pressure to that mountain until it is gone forever. Believe me, it works!

Not too long ago a woman from my congregation decided she had had enough of struggling to make ends meet. She was fed up with having to pay a car note, mortgage, and other monthly obligations. She never seemed to have enough left over between pay periods. She bought a large poster board, drew several mountains, and labeled each one with a debt she owed. Every day, several times a day, she would recite aloud the names of her creditors and the amounts owed to each one; she then ended her confession time by praising and thanking God for her debt deliverance before she saw anything happen. It wasn't long before every single debt had been paid off! She is now debt free and able to work because she wants to, not because she has to.

4. Don't cancel out what you confess.

You must be careful not to cancel out your positive confessions with negative ones. By the same token, you must refuse to listen to anything negative. Instead, focus your attention on aligning your words with God's Word. Ephesians 4:29 tells us to *"Let no corrupt communication proceed out of your mouth, but that which is good to the use of edifying, that it may minister grace to the hearers."* And again in Philippians 4:8 Paul tells us to think on things that are true, honest, just, pure, lovely, of good report, virtuous, and praiseworthy.

For example, if you're praying for a $10,000 increase on your job, don't turn around and say, "My boss will never give me the raise I need." You see, just as God and the angels begin setting things in motion for your specific request for a pay raise, you'll go and cancel the order with your negative confessions. Remember, confessions can be positive or negative. But only positive confessions based on God's Word will cancel your debt.

This principle is important because what you meditate on in your heart is what will come out of your mouth (Matthew 12:34; Proverbs 23:7). Instead of confessing what things may seem like or feel like, try confessing how you would like things to be. The Word says that we can speak, or call forth those things that have yet to manifest as if they were already in existence (Romans 4:17). This does not mean that we deny what's present; rather, by faith we confess the desired result. Why waste time talking about "what is" when you could be planting seeds of faith in your heart for what you truly desire? Use the Word of God to guide your declarations of faith. And guard your heart carefully, because it is the control center of your life (Proverbs 4:23).

5. Bind the strong man.

Debt is a demonic spirit designed to keep you from experiencing the abundant life Jesus promised in John 10:10. *The Amplified Bible* version of Proverbs 22:7 tells us that *"...the borrower is servant to the lender."* Debt comes from the strong man, Satan, who desires for you to remain in bondage. He must be bound up so that you can walk in your God-given inheritance of prosperity, divine health, protection, and heavenly provision. Mark 3:27 says, *"No man can enter into a strong man's house, and spoil his goods, except he will first bind the strong man; and then he will spoil his house."* On the other hand, you must also loose God and His angels to bring about your debt cancellation. Command the angels of God to go forth and bring in your harvest!

Satan is a thief. Proverbs 6:31 tells us that when the thief is found, he must return what he has stolen seven times over. As a result, you must let him know, once and for all, that he will no longer be allowed to operate in your finances. Do this as often as necessary—especially on those days when it seems as if he's got the victory. Remember that the Word of God and the name of Jesus are stronger than any demonic spirit. First John 4:4 says, *"...greater is he that is in you, than he that is in the world."*

6. Become a tither in a Word-based local church and obey God in your giving.

Malachi 3:8-10 makes it very clear that if you are not tithing, you are stealing from God. In light of all He has done and continues to do for you, ten percent of your income is not too much to ask. This is a small amount of seed that goes to managing His house—the church. In addition, the tithe is your covenant connector. It keeps the windows of heaven open over your life and activates the blessings and promises of God. You cannot expect supernatural debt cancellation if you refuse to obey God with your tithe.

In addition, you cannot just tithe anywhere. You must be sure to sow your seed in a Word-based ministry that faithfully obeys God's instructions. And when you tithe, pray over your seed! Command it to go and grow in Jesus' name and say aloud the specific harvest you desire for that seed. This is what I call "tithing the tithe." It's okay to expect God to move on your behalf. The tithe connects you to His promises of total life prosperity; therefore, write down what you are believing God for on your tithe envelope, declare those debt-canceling scriptures aloud, and expect supernatural results!

You must also obey God in your giving. This means whenever and whatever He tells you to sow, do so with a cheerful heart! Don't allow the devil or the opinions and traditions of men to keep you from being the blessing God desires you to be. Purpose in your heart to allow God to control your finances. Through your obedience, you leave the door wide open for Him to cancel your debt in an instant.

✗   ✗   ✗   ✗

As you apply these simple principles to your life, expect the miracle of debt cancellation to manifest. Matthew 19:26 tells us that *"...with God all things are possible."* Remember to walk in confidence because God delights in your prosperity. He is a miracle-working, debt-canceling God, and as His child, you are entitled to walk in the freedom of God's manifested abundance, today.

4

The Building Blocks
of Debt Cancellation

Chapter 4

The Building Blocks of Debt Cancellation

"...But let every man take heed how he buildeth...For other foundation can no man lay than that is laid..." (1 Corinthians 3:10,11).

G etting out of debt is like building a house. You have to gather all of the materials together before you begin. It's a waste of time to start something and then have to stop because you don't have the necessary supplies to finish the job. Luke 14:28-30 says, *"For which of you, intending to build a tower, sitteth not down first, and counteth the cost, whether he have sufficient to finish it? Lest haply, after he hath laid the foundation, and is not able to finish it, all that behold it begin to mock him, Saying, This man began to build, and was not able to finish."* In other words, think about what you want to do and what it will cost you personally to do it.

Most people begin the process of debt release without considering the amount of work involved. They love to shout "money cometh," but when they realize there's a price to pay for debt release, they quit. It's not fair for you to expect something for nothing. God doesn't work that way. The law of sowing and reaping in Galatians 6:7 makes it pretty clear that you must plant the right seeds in order to reap the right harvest. If you want a harvest of debt release, guess what? You'll have to plant seeds of debt release.

Created In His Image

The great thing about life is that no matter what situation or circumstance you find yourself in, there is always a way out. Paul tells us in 1 Corinthians 10:13

that God *"...is faithful, who will not suffer you to be tempted above that ye are able; but will...make a way to escape...."* In other words, God has given you the tools to get whatever it is you need. But it's up to you to use them. And the most powerful tool at your disposal is found less than 2 inches from the tip of your nose—your mouth.

When God made man in Genesis Chapter 1, He gave him two things: His authority and His ability to create. No other creature on the planet can do what man can do. Why? We were created in God's image—right down to our ability to create something from nothing. In other words, we were created with the power to reshape our situations and circumstances, just like God. If you read through the first chapter of Genesis, you'll see two things. First, God spoke what He wanted to happen; and second, it happened. All the way through you'll read the words *"And God said..."* (Genesis 1:9,11,14,20,24,26,29). Then in verse 31 you'll read the words, *"And God saw."* He literally spoke the entire world into being.

Everything that exists has its origin in God. John

1:1-3 tells us, "*In the beginning was the Word, and the Word was with God, and the Word was God. The same was in the beginning with God. All things were made by him; and without him was not any thing made that was made.*" Notice the word *all*. God didn't create the animal and plant kingdom and then leave mankind to the process of evolution. No, He spoke everything into existence. He took invisible matter and made it visible. He used spiritual building blocks to manifest what He wanted in the physical realm.

It's important to realize that before anything can materialize in this physical realm, it had to have its origin in the spirit realm. Genesis 1:2 says "*...the earth was without form, and void; and darkness was upon the face of the deep. And the Spirit of God moved upon the face of the waters.*" There was no light at all. So what did God do? He spoke it into existence. "*...Let there be light...*" (v.3). He pulled something from the spiritual, or invisible realm, and commanded it to manifest itself. What happened? The Bible says, "*...and there was light*" (v.3). Incredibly enough, the light—the sun, moon, and stars—came into being.

Follow God's Example

In order to get out of debt, you must follow God's example in Genesis Chapter 1 and call things that are not as though they were (Romans 4:17). You've got to speak up and use spiritual material in order to bring about a physical manifestation. In other words, you must get the Word of God on it. Create a list of scriptures that support what you're believing God for and begin to say them aloud daily, several times a day. Your spiritual building blocks must come straight out of the Bible. You just can't claim debt release without anything to back it up. In Isaiah 55:11, God tells us His Word will not return void, but will always achieve the purpose for which it was sent. Nowhere in that scripture does it say your words will achieve anything. It's God's Word that changes things. Believe me, confessions work!

Your faith is the "title deed," or assurance, for debt release. *"Now faith is the assurance (the confirmation, the title deed) of the things [we] hope for, being the proof of things [we] do not see..."* (Hebrews 11:1, *AMP*). Now a title deed signifies two things. First, it indicates that something does exist; and second, that someone owns it. For example, every car on the road today has an owner. But that doesn't necessarily mean the person driving the car owns the vehicle. More than likely the finance company holds the title.

A deed is never drawn up for something that doesn't exist. That's ridiculous. And so is claiming ownership of something you don't have the deed for. Unfortunately, this is exactly what many Christians do when they confess debt release. They have failed to build their faith up to the point where they have assurance that they will indeed receive what they are confessing. In the words of my wife, Taffi, "You're not creating anything if you're not saying anything."

The Bible is our book of title deeds. It covers everything from prosperity and debt cancellation to healing, restoration, deliverance, salvation, and long life. Your Bible is the cornerstone of whatever you need from God. A *cornerstone* is "a basic element or foundation." It strengthens whatever you're trying to build. The prophet Isaiah spoke of Jesus as *"...a precious cornerstone, a sure foundation..."* that undergirds the members of His Body (Isaiah 28:16). The Word strengthens your confessions because you are now using God's words instead of your own.

Deposit the Word in Your Heart

It is absolutely vital that you begin depositing the Word of God in your heart daily. Proverbs 4:20,21 commands you to keep the Word in your heart. That means actually digging into Scripture to find the material you need to build a way out of your circumstances. However, it's not enough to just know where the scriptures are. You must meditate on them and confess them several times a day in order to receive your manifestation.

Romans 10:17 says *"...faith cometh by hearing, and hearing by the word of God."* Your faith cannot be built on thoughts. Paul said that faith is built up by hearing the Word of God. When you give voice to the

Word, you are actually writing it on your heart. By combining belief with action you increase your level of confidence. The more you confess your debt release, the faster it becomes *rhema,* or real, to you. Once this has occurred, *patience*, or "the ability to be constant, consistent, and stable," can come in and do its perfect work in you. In other words, the confidence you develop in God and His Word empowers you to wait expectantly for the manifestation of your miracle.

It is important that you diligently guard the title deeds you've deposited in your heart. It only takes a moment for Satan to tear down what God had taken time to build in you. Doubt, fear, neglect, and complacency are subtle weapons of the enemy that act like wrecking balls to destroy your faith. But by not letting your guard down, you keep your faith level high and your mind focused on God, thereby overcoming the pitiful attacks of the enemy.

To get you started on the road to debt release, I have listed several keys.

1. Diligently search Scripture for your title deeds.

You must have the Word of God to back up your claims. It gives the Holy Spirit something to work with. In Isaiah 43:26, God commanded us to remind Him of His promises to us. You just can't claim something without the proof that it's yours. In Galatians 3:29, Paul tells us that we are seeds of Abraham and heirs according to the promise. That means everything promised to Abraham belongs to us—long life, health, peace, prosperity, salvation, and deliverance. But unless you diligently study the Word, you'll never know what God has set aside for you to have. Your inheritance is listed in Deuteronomy 28:1-14. When in doubt, check the Word. If God's Word says it, you can have it.

2. Write the scriptures down.

Habakkuk 2:2 commands us to *"...Write the vision, and make it plain...that he may run that readeth it."* This is your safeguard against forgetting. Writing down your supporting scriptures concerning your debt and God's promises keeps your mind focused and your faith level up. But it only works when you post them someplace where you'll see them. It does you no good to keep them tucked away in your Bible or anyplace else where you're likely to forget about them. Post them beside your computer at work, in your car, or on your refrigerator. The more you see them, the more real they will be to you, which will increase your levels of expectation and confidence.

3. Say them aloud several times a day.

Prayer involves more than just mumbling a few broken phrases or presenting God with a list of your needs and desires; instead, it is simply repeating back to God what He has already promised you in His Word. When you boldly declare your right to those title deeds, you give power and authority to what you say. Why? God's Word is His voice, and all creation makes the necessary adjustments to bring His Word to pass.

This is the point where faith and belief divide. Belief says, "I know God wants to give me a house.

Faith says, "I *will* have a house, because such-and-such scripture tells me so." It's not enough to think or know what God's Word says. You must act on your faith in order to receive it. Faith is the key to getting things manifested in the physical realm. Here's a simple formula to remember:

God's Word (title deed) + action (confession)= manifestation (your request)

4. Let patience do its work.

Have you ever heard the phrase, "A watched pot never boils"? If you keep lifting the lid off the kettle as the water is trying to boil, you will constantly let the steam out of the pot. In the end it will take longer for the water to boil. That principle can also be applied to the spiritual realm. It takes a little time to receive the manifestation of what you're confessing daily. Why? Think of words as seeds. When you plant corn in the field, does it come up overnight? Of course not! The same is true with the confessions you make. God's Word is incorruptible seed that needs time to grow roots, mature, and sprout.

The words you speak must be rhema to you before anything can happen. That's when patience steps in and says, "No matter what it looks like, sounds like, feels like, or seems like, I'll have what I say. I am a child of God, and I cannot be denied!" Don't try to speed up the process, because only God knows how, when and where you'll receive your manifestation. Your job is to continue to make your declarations concerning debt release boldly and consistently.

5. Guard your mouth.

Once you've begun to put God's Word in your heart and on your tongue, you must avoid speaking things that will cancel out your confessions. That means not allowing anything negative to come out of your mouth. For example, "I'm broke," "I'll never get out of debt," or "Confessions don't work." Don't allow your mouth to get you in trouble. That's often the biggest reason for a delay in manifestation. You really never know how close you are to receiving what you've been believing God for, and if you open your mouth and begin to confess things that are negative, it's more than likely you'll end up back at square one.

Manifestation Awaits You

It is impossible to make anything without the right materials. Every project requires an assessment of what is needed to accomplish the job. The Word of God is the basic building block for everything in life. Without it, nothing comes to pass. Hebrews 11:3 states that everything we see was made out of material we cannot see. In other words, the invisible power of God's Word pulls things out of the spiritual realm, or the invisible world, and brings them into the natural, or visible world around us.

✗   ✗   ✗   ✗

What have you been trying to build, but have yet to see? Perhaps you have been using the wrong materials. Or maybe you've had the right material all along, but you just haven't been using it consistently. Whatever the reason, it's time for you to diligently apply yourself to the task. Begin right now to open your mouth and proclaim your right to the title deeds outlined in the Word concerning your debt deliverance. Build yourself up to receive whatever it is you need from God. Your manifestation awaits you.

Daily Confessions

Listed below are specific confessions to assist you in making your debt freedom a reality. Recite them aloud daily, and add others to them. Don't forget to be specific! Remember, God is willing and able to give you your heart's desire and perform your miracle of debt release today.

✗   ✗   ✗   ✗

1. Psalm 35:27 says God delights in the prosperity of His servants. Therefore, as His servant, I declare that I am out of debt, my needs are met, and I have plenty more to put in store.

2. I no longer operate by the world's system of debt cancellation, but by God's system of seedtime and harvest (Galatians 6:7,9). I believe that when I sow seed into good ground, I reap an immediate, hundred-fold return.

3. I am a cheerful giver, and I sow under the direction of the Holy Spirit (2 Corinthians 9:7).

4. I have a hearing heart because I meditate on God's Word daily. As a result, I hear God's voice clearly and operate in His wisdom and anointing (Isaiah 30:21).

5. Proverbs 4:23 says that out of the heart flow the issues of life. Therefore, I refuse to allow anything to come before my eyes, in my ears or out of my mouth that does not line up with the Word of God. I purpose to guard my heart diligently by bringing every thought, action or desire into submission to the Word (2 Corinthians 10:5).

6. As I continue to speak debt-canceling scriptures over my finances (Psalm 103:20), I command the angels of God to go forth NOW and bring in my promotion and increase in Jesus' name!

5

A Partner With the Anointing

Chapter 5

A Partner With the Anointing

"...Stand fast in one spirit, with one mind striving together for the faith of the gospel" (Philippians 1:27).

S omething extraordinary happens when you decide to partner, or work closely with, the anointing. The anointing is the burden-removing, yoke-destroying power of God given to Jesus in Luke 4:18. Before departing from the earth, Jesus promised that we would be able to do greater works than Him (John 14:12). By utilizing the anointing, you unleash the power of agreement over areas in your life where there may be sin, lack, or confusion, enabling you to supernaturally overcome them. Simply put, you allow the power of God to step in and change your circumstances.

By partnering with the anointing, you partake of all the benefits that come with it—healing, prosperity, wisdom, deliverance, salvation, and restoration. You may be thinking, "But Brother Dollar, how is it possible to partner with the anointing? You can't really see it. It's not a person." Well, it may not be a person, but it is designed to operate through people just as it did through Jesus. Ephesians 4:11-13 tells us that we have been given apostles, prophets, pastors, teachers, and evangelists—anointed men and women of God—so that the Body of Christ may be edified and matured. The Bible refers to them as ministry gifts. They are our bridges to God. And by partnering with them, you join forces with the burden-removing, yoke-destroying power on their lives.

Of course, not everyone who claims to be anointed is. You can't judge by outward appearances. God rebuked the prophet Samuel for doing just that. Samuel thought that God had chosen Eliab, David's older brother, to be king over Israel. But God told him, "...Look not on his countenance, or on the height of his *stature; because I have refused him: for the Lord seeth not as man seeth; for man looketh on the outward appearance, but the Lord looketh on the heart"* (1 Samuel 16:7). You can't become a partner with someone just because they dress well or you see them on television. There must be visible, tangible proof that God is using them to remove burdens and destroy yokes.

A Covenant Relationship

It's important to understand that true partnership is not just saying you are someone's partner. It is a covenant relationship, which means there are certain responsibilities that come with it. For example, when I send material to my ministry partners, I outline the responsibilities we have toward one another.

Our part is to:

- Pray daily for God's blessings to be upon you.
- Study the Word and diligently seek God on
  your behalf.

- Minister to you monthly in a personal letter.
- Furnish an official Vision Partner Kit.
- Periodically offer special gifts for your spiritual edification and growth.

Your part is to:

- Always pray for Creflo Dollar Ministries.
- Be committed to support *Changing Your World* meetings in your area.
- Support the ministry financially with your monthly pledge (Philippians 4:17).
- Consistently lift up the ministry, Dr. Dollar, and his family with positive confessions.

Notice that partnership involves financial giving. Sowing financial seed into good ground puts pressure on the anointing that is on that man or woman of God. In other words, your giving obligates God to work on your behalf. Therefore, He has to recompense you for the seed you sow. But you must plant the right kind of seed to reap the correct harvest. In this case you want to reap debt release. It's impossible to plant corn seeds and get blueberries. You must plant corn to get corn. The same is true in the spiritual realm. If you sow money toward someone else's debt release, you'll reap money for your debt release. That's God method of doing things. So if you want to get out of debt, you'll have to sow debt-canceling seeds—money.

Sadly, many Christians see financial giving as a loss. It grieves them to give. It grieves them to tithe. They are under the mistaken impression that if they give to a man or woman of God, they're being robbed. "Well, I knew that Creflo Dollar person was after my money. That's all he ever talks about!" Child of God, I'm not trying to take something from you; instead, I'm trying to get something to you! I'm trying to position you to receive whatever it is you need from God. It's not enough to give a dollar here and there, and then expect a hundred-fold return. That's like planting a handful of seed on a thousand-acre farm and expecting it to grow without first testing the soil to see if it's good!

Anointed to Bless You

God uses anointed men and women to bridge

the gap between your need and His abundance. That's the way the system is set up. In fact, every financial miracle outlined in the Bible has a man or woman of God as its central figure.

2 Kings 4:1-7

Now there cried a certain woman of the wives of the sons of the prophets unto Elisha, saying, Thy servant my husband is dead; and thou knowest that thy servant did fear the Lord: and the creditor is come to take unto him my two sons to be bondmen. And Elisha said unto her, What shall I do for thee? tell me, what hast thou in the house? And she said, Thine handmaid hath not any thing in the house, save a pot of oil. Then he said, Go, borrow thee vessels abroad of all thy neighbors, even empty vessels; borrow not a few. And when thou art come in, thou shalt shut the door upon thee and upon thy sons, and shalt pour out into all those vessels, and thou shalt set aside that which is full. So she went from him, and shut the door upon her and upon her sons, who brought the vessels to her, and she poured out. And it came to pass, when the vessels were full, that she said unto her son, Bring me yet a vessel. And he said unto her, There is not a vessel more. And the oil stayed. Then she came and told the man of God. And he said,

Go, sell the oil, and pay thy debt, and live thou and thy children of the rest.

This was a woman in trouble. Her husband was still in debt when he died, and his creditors wanted to add insult to injury by enslaving her sons. So what did she do? Have a pity party? Leave town in the middle of the night? Auction off her children? No! Instead, she called on Elisha, the prophet of God, who told her what to do. By presenting her case to him, she put a demand on the anointings of wisdom and counsel that were present in his life, and it brought about her financial miracle. What would have happened if the widow had excluded the man of God? More than likely she would have remained in debt, and the creditors would've taken her sons away from her.

The anointing that is present in the lives of true men and women of God is not there just for them but for you. Of course, they get blessed. That comes with the territory. Proverbs 11:25 says he who refreshes others will also be refreshed. That's a positive aspect. However, the real focus is on whom the anointing is helping, not through whom it flows. That's why partnership is so important. You are not joining forces with a person as much as with the power that works in and through them.

Take, for example, the Shunammite woman mentioned later on in 2 Kings 4. She rightly *perceived,* or "was aware of," the anointing on Elisha's life. Because of this, she gave him food and water in addition to his own room in her house (vv. 9,10). In other words, she sowed a seed into his life. As a result, the man of God blessed her, and she conceived a son. Remember, to *bless* means "to empower to prosper and excel." Having a son was the one thing she desired most in the world. Ironically, although she had been aware of Elisha's anointing, she was completely unaware of the amount of seed she had sown into his life. It was only after her son died that she realized she could place a demand on that seed. Consequently, she called upon the man of God to supernaturally revive her child. As a result, God recompensed her by providing a way for the child to live.

What stood between the Shunammite's desire

and the manifestation of it? The anointing on the man of God. Here is where many of us miss the mark. Instead of allowing God to direct us on where we should sow our seed, we give blindly out of emotion or even ignorance. We don't take the time to observe whether or not the anointing is present on their lives. The Shunammite woman knew better. She had observed Elisha *"...as oft as he passed by..."* (2 Kings 4:8). The root word *observe* means "to watch carefully with attention to detail or behavior for the purpose of arriving at a judgment." In other words, the Shunammite woman watched Elisha for signs of the power of God. Then she chose to sow into the anointing she had observed on his life.

Your Seed Applies Faith Pressure

Becoming a partner with the anointing is not about giving money away. You don't lose anything when you sow into the Kingdom of God system. Instead, your seed applies faith pressure to get whatever you need from God. Realize that you must sow a seed in order to release the anointing. This principle is illustrated in the book of John.

John 6:5-13

When Jesus then lifted up his eyes, and saw a great company come unto him, he saith unto Philip, Whence shall we buy bread, that these may eat? And this he said to prove him: for he himself knew what he would do...One of his disciples, Andrew, Simon Peter's brother, saith unto him, There is a lad here, which hath five barley loaves, and two small fishes: but what are they among so many? And Jesus said, Make the men sit down. Now there was much grass in the place. So the men sat down, in number about five thousand. And Jesus took the loaves; and when he had given thanks, he distributed to the disciples, and the disciples to them that were set down; and likewise of the fishes as much as they would. When they were filled, he said unto his disciples, Gather up the fragments that remain, that nothing be lost. Therefore they gathered them together, and filled twelve baskets with the fragments of the five barley loaves, which

*remained over and above unto them that
had eaten.*

Here we see Jesus feeding not only five thousand men, but their families as well. It's safe to say that there were over 10,000 people present on the hill that day. The disciples were clueless as to how they were going to feed so many people with only five loaves and two fish. How many could that feed? But take a look at what happened. The two-piece fish dinner became a meal big enough to feed an army. How? The owner of that dinner sowed a seed into the anointing on Jesus' life by giving Him his meal. As a result, that anointing multiplied the seed until the insufficiency was wiped out. In fact, there were twelve baskets of leftovers for that boy to carry home to his mother. What stood between the need and the provision? The man of God.

You see, God will always recompense you for your seed. Proverbs 18:16 states that *"A man's gift maketh room for him, and bringeth him before great men."* In Hebrew, the word *gift* means "money." In other words, your money makes room for you. Room for what? Room for more of whatever is missing in your life. The Queen of Sheba would know. She sowed millions of dollars into Solomon's life after just one visit with him. Why? She rightly perceived his anointing—the anointing of wisdom, knowledge, counsel, and prosperity. Even Solomon himself knew the benefits of sowing into the anointing. The Bible tells us that after offering a thousand burnt offerings, God spoke to him in a dream that very night, and he received much more than he had asked for (2 Chronicles 1:6-12).

Child of God, you can't allow your present circumstances to dictate what you should or should not sow. I have yet to meet one person who couldn't give me a testimony of a situation where they didn't have enough to pay their monthly obligations. But I know of a few believers who took what they had— even if it was just $2.50—and sowed it into the kingdom of God with great success.

Don't minimize the amount you can give. It could be a few cents or a few hundred dollars. The truth of the matter is, regardless of the amount, any sacrificial offering given with the right attitude is a debt canceling seed! What would have happened if that boy had said, "I can't give you my dinner, Jesus? I know you want to feed all these people, but I don't have enough for them and me." More than likely Jesus would have found another way to feed the 5,000. But that boy and his family would have missed out on their opportunity to be blessed to be a blessing (Genesis 12:2).

A Fail-Proof System

The Kingdom of God system—seedtime and harvest time—is a fail-proof system. It is guaranteed to bring results every time you use it. Do you remember the widow with the cruse of oil in 1 Kings 17? When Elisha found her, she was gathering sticks in order to cook her last meal. She had no money and very little food left, only *"...a handful of meal in a barrel, and a little oil in a cruse..."* (v.12). What happened? Elisha instructed her to *"...Fear not; go and do as thou hast said: but make me thereof a little cake first, and bring it unto me, and after make for thee and for thy son"* (v.13).

Notice that the first thing he told her to do was to *"...Fear not...."* Why? Fear hinders your harvest. You cannot be afraid of what people are going to say when you decide to sow your seed into good ground. There will always be opposition from the enemy concerning God's method for debt cancellation. However, you cannot be swayed by every wind that blows. The Word of God must be your final authority for everything in life. When it is, you will be able to withstand the attack of the enemy.

Second, the man of God commanded the widow to first make him a cake before she made one for herself and her son. Can you imagine the type of press Elijah would have received if someone had found out his request? More than likely the headlines would have read, "MEAN PROPHET TAKES WIDOW-WOMAN'S LAST MEAL." In spite of his seemingly unrealistic request, the woman did as she was told. And what happened? The woman, her family, and the prophet were able to eat for many days (v.15). This woman had a choice. She could have chosen to ignore the man of God, and starved to death as a result. Instead, she put the little that she had into his hands, and the anointing ensured that she had more than enough to meet her need.

Most people are not desperate enough to trust God. They're too busy fluctuating between God's way and the world's way of getting out of debt. That's what the Bible calls being double-minded. The book of James tells us that a double-minded man is unstable in all he does. In other words, he is easily persuaded. You see, the world's system will fail you every time, because as a child of God, you are no longer equipped to operate by the world's standards. That system is designed to keep you in debt. God's way—although it may seem strange—is the best way. The Word of God tells us that God has used the foolish things of the world to shame the "wise" (1 Corinthians 1:27). In other words, He uses the very thing you disregard to get you out of debt, like that two-piece fish dinner.

Make the Word Your Final Authority

It's important to remember that you cannot do

anything aside from the Word of God, including sowing seed. You can't sow your seed just because someone else says it works, although that can be very encouraging to hear. You must sow into the anointing because you find it in the Word. If you read back over all of the examples used in this chapter, you'll find that in each case the blessings came through the prophet at the command of God.

The key to manifestation lies in your decision to make the Word the final authority in your life. You must believe God and His Word so that you can be established, or unwavering, in the things of God. If you don't know the value of partnering with the anointing, then you'll never be able to sow a seed into the lives of anointed men and women of God.

x   x   x   x

If we're going to reach the financial realm God desires for us to live in during these last days, we're going to have to stop depending on the world's resources and turn to what is available through the anointing of God. Purpose in your heart to seek direction on where God would have you to sow, and then do it willingly. Allow your seed to put faith pressure on the burden-removing, yoke-destroying power of God, and watch the manifestation of abundance pour into your life.

6
Entertaining Angels

Chapter 6

Entertaining Angels

"Bless the Lord, ye his angels, that excel in strength, that do his commandments, hearkening unto the voice of his word. Bless ye the Lord, all ye his hosts; ye ministers of his, that do his pleasure" (Psalm 103:20,21).

I love testimonies. I like nothing better than to hear how a person's life has been changed for the better because of the Word of God. That's why I'm always encouraging partners, supporters, friends, and members to send me their testimonies. Over the years I've received some pretty incredible accounts—some of which have even been accompanied by photographs of the supernatural. Photographs of things like angels. Yes, angels.

Now, there are some people who don't believe in angels, but I know better. I've had too many personal experiences to argue about whether or not they exist. For example, when I was a first year student attending college in West Virginia, I nearly ran off the road when my car hit a bad spot and began to skid. At the time I thought, "This is it!" and prepared myself for the worst. However, as soon as my car began to run off the road, I felt "something" pushing it back to where it was supposed to be. It really woke me up. There was no way I could have saved myself. There wasn't any time for me to do anything. The only explanation I could come up with was a supernatural one. That incident marked the beginning of God's call on my life.

Created for a Purpose

Of course, even in spite of testimonies such as these, there are still people out there who refuse to believe. On the other hand, however, there are those who believe in angels to the point of worshipping them. Angels were never meant to be worshipped. Instead, they were created with a specific purpose in mind—to serve God and His people. Hebrews 1:14 tells us angels are *"...all ministering spirits, sent forth to minister for them who shall be heirs of salvation."* In other words, their job is to minister, or serve God's people. Notice the phrase, *"...who shall be heirs of salvation."* The Greek word for *salvation* is translated *soteria,* which means "deliverance, safety, protection, provision, soundness, and prosperity." If you are born again, you are an heir to all of these things. However, it's not just a one-time deal. According to this definition, salvation does not just mean being born again; rather, it implies an on-going process whereby you continually receive deliverance, safety, protection, provision, soundness, and prosperity. And angels are the unseen workers that help to bring these promises of soteria to pass in your life.

The Bible is full of references concerning angels. They rescued Lot (Genesis 19:1-29), Daniel (Daniel

6:1-23), Peter (Acts 12:1-19), and Shadrach, Meshach, and Abednego (Daniel 3:1-28). It was the angel Gabriel who told Mary she would conceive supernaturally (Luke 1:26-38). Daniel received the answer to His prayers from an angel after 21 days of heavenly warfare (Daniel 10:7-21). A multitude of angels announced the birth of Christ to shepherds in a field (Luke 2:8-15). And they also ministered to Jesus after His ordeal in the wilderness (Matthew 4:1-11).

There are millions of angels in heaven. Each one has a specific job to do. Some are messengers. Some simply praise and worship God continually. And still others fight the demonic forces around us. Revelation 5:11 tells us that there are tens of thousands of angels in existence today. That may very well mean that every person on this earth has over 100 angels. And most people only believe they have one guardian angel!

Angels Are Important

Why are angels so important to your debt

deliverance? It's simple. They are the unseen forces that make it happen. Let me explain. God designed angels to perform certain tasks for His people. Their primary function is to carry out and establish the Word of God. Psalm 103:20 says, *"Bless the Lord, ye his angels, that excel in strength, that do his commandments, hearkening unto the voice of his word."* The word *hearken* means to "listen and obey." In other words, angels listen and obey the spoken Word of God. When you confess scriptures on debt deliverance, you are speaking the Word over that particular situation. That is what causes the heavenly host to move on your behalf. God is not moved by need, but by faith. You can shout, scream, dance, cry, and beg; however, unless you are confidently speaking what God's Word has to say about debt and debt cancellation, nothing will change.

Angels have not been programmed to recognize anyone else's authority except God's. They only obey what He commands them to do. John 1:1 tells us that the Word is God. When you speak the Word, you speak with God's authority. It's as if He were the One speaking instead of you. For example, there is a strong bond between mother and child. A mother knows her child and can distinguish his or her cry from the cry of another baby. If you were to put her child in a room full of crying babies, she could hear her child above all the rest. Why? Her ear is trained to recognize the sound of her baby's voice. The same is true in the spirit realm. Angels have been trained to only recognize the voice of God. You can quote a million things that sound like Scripture, but unless you speak the Word, your angels will not move on your behalf. They just don't know any other way of working.

A Helping Hand

Why would God choose to employ angels on our behalf? There are times when we need direction or a little added assurance in our walk of faith. For example, Joseph, Mary's husband, was shocked to hear his fiancée was pregnant. He was not privy to the conversation she had had with the angel, Gabriel, and was not aware that the pregnancy was supernatural.

All he knew was that she was engaged to marry him, and now she was pregnant with someone else's baby. As a result, he decided to break off the engagement; however, God had something else in mind for him.

> Matthew 1:19-24
>
> *Then Joseph her husband, being a just man, and not willing to make her a public example was minded to put her away privily. But while he thought on these things, behold, the angel of the Lord appeared unto him in a dream, saying, Joseph, thou son of David, fear not to take unto thee Mary thy wife: for that which is conceived in her is of the Holy Ghost. And she shall bring forth a son, and thou shalt call his name JESUS: for he shall save his people from their sins...Then Joseph being raised from sleep did as the angel of the Lord had bidden him, and took unto him his wife....*

If you continue reading the scripture, you'll find that the same angel spoke to Joseph again, directing him to another city. Without this angelic intervention, Joseph would have either sent Mary away, or married her and lost the baby to Herod's army.

We don't always have to hear from angels

before we believe that God will work things out for us. It's just that every once in a while our faith needs a little boost, so God sets up a divine encounter to help us out.

Enforcers of the Covenant

The primary function of angels is to enforce the mandate given to Abraham in Genesis 12:3—to be blessed to be a blessing until all families of the earth have been blessed. In other words, they are to enforce the blessings of prosperity God spoke over Abraham's life. As Abraham's descendants (Galatians 3:29), we must be committed to seeing this promise manifest in our lives. That's why it's so important that we get out of debt and stay out. It's impossible to be a blessing to another person when your hands are tied financially. As the Body of Christ, we have an obligation to prosper and increase in all that we do. That's called good stewardship. Remember the men with the talents? The one who multiplied his money received more, while the one who hid it was cast into utter darkness

(Matthew 25:14-30). When you are a good steward, or manager, of God's money, He sees to it that you are given more and more.

Galatians 3:18,19 makes it very clear that angels administer the covenant promises of Abraham. "...*But God gave it to Abraham by promise. Wherefore then serveth the law? It was added because of transgressions, till the seed should come to whom the promise was made; and it was ordained by angels....*" The word *ordained* means "to administer, manage, conduct, furnish, supply, dispense, or execute," or "to have charge of as chief agent in managing." Angels ensure that we have everything we need to be a blessing to others.

Confidence is the Key

When you speak the Word of God over your financial situation, you loose the angels of God to work on your behalf. They immediately hear the voice of God speaking through you, and they rush to obey. It's that simple. You don't have to dance, cry, or beg. The Word of God is power enough to send the heavenly host to the four corners of the earth. The only thing you have to do is put your trust in God and His Word. Confidence is the key to motivating your angels. It does you no good to declare God's Word when you don't believe it will do what it claims it can.

So how do you build your confidence level and employ angels to assist in your debt deliverance? It's simple. Study and meditate on God's Word. You must believe, beyond a shadow of a doubt, that God desires for you to prosper in every area of your life and that He has given *"...his angels charge over thee, to keep thee in all thy ways"* (Psalm 91:11). Isaiah 55:11 tells us that the spoken Word *"...shall not return unto me void, but it shall accomplish that which I please...."* The more you meditate on God's Word, the more confident you'll become in His promises, and the faster your angels will work on your behalf.

Employ Your Angels With the Word

Command your angels to carry out assignments daily concerning your debt deliverance. Through God, they can do miraculous things. While you're asleep at night, they're on assignment at the mortgage company reducing your bottom line, or at the bank taking care of your student loans, car payments, and credit card bills. It's important to remember that you have an invisible heavenly army working on your behalf. You have more angels working for you in the unseen realm than you have options in the natural realm.

✗   ✗   ✗   ✗

Don't put your confidence in people, institutions, or the world's system to bring about your debt deliverance, because they will always let you down. Instead, put your faith and trust in God and His Word and the system He has designed to bring you out of debt. You will not be disappointed!

7
Weapons of
Warfare

Chapter 7

Weapons of Warfare

"For though we walk in the flesh, we do not war after the flesh: (For the weapons of our warfare are not carnal, but mighty through God to the pulling down of strongholds;)..." (2 Corinthians 10:3,4).

W hen you think about waging war against an adversary, you don't exactly imagine yourself using invisible weapons. Instead, you pull out the heavy machinery like tanks, surface-to-air missiles, fighter jets, and rapid-fire guns. I don't know of one person who could imagine himself standing in front of enemy fire armed only with an invisible gun and a steely determination to win. But that's exactly what the Bible counsels us to do—use God's "invisible" weapons of joy and praise to defeat Satan and secure victory in our everyday lives. Therefore, I recommend using these same forces in your war against debt. In the end, you'll win.

We are warned in 1 Peter 5:8 to *"Be sober, be vigilant; because your adversary the devil, as a roaring lion, walketh about, seeking whom he may devour...."* In other words, Satan masquerades himself as a powerful figure, but is really nothing more than a pretender whose only weapons are fear and intimidation. Unfortunately, that's enough to send most Christians running for the hills. Examine yourself for a moment. When you are under spiritual attack, what is the first thing you do? Complain? Feel sorry for yourself? Wonder what you've done to deserve the attack? Or do you rejoice and stand your ground through the promises of God's Word? According to 2 Peter 1:3, God has placed within us *"...all things that pertain unto life and godliness...."* In other words, we've been given everything we need—tools, weapons, and ideas—to overcome the enemy and experience abundant life. It's up to us to tap into those resources and get results.

From the Natural to the Spiritual

Joy and praise are two of the most powerful weapons in God's arsenal. Together they form a protective barrier against demonic attack. How? They are designed to make you rely more on God's strength than on your own. You see, the devil knows that in order to win a battle, he must first take your responses out of the spiritual realm and bring them into the natural. He wants you to respond in the flesh rather than by the Spirit of God. For example, let's say you are driving home from work one evening and someone cuts you off—another centimeter to the right and this person would have smashed the front of your car. What do you do? I know what my initial reaction may have been in the past—blow the horn, roll down the window, and let that driver have it! But that's a fleshly response to the situation and exactly what Satan wants us to do. Thank God for a renewed mind!

You must understand that the enemy is capable of using the people around you to get you to respond in a way that damages your Christian witness and brings shame to God. And it's equally important to remember that they are not your real enemies—Satan is. You should not make the mistake of fighting people, because that's also what the enemy wants. He desires for you to forget about the invisible and concentrate on the visible. The Bible warns us about this in Ephesians 6:12. *"For we wrestle not against flesh and blood, but against principalities, against powers, against the rulers of the darkness of this world, against spiritual wickedness in high places."*

Now, armed with this understanding, let's turn that "road rage" situation around. What do you think would happen if, instead of honking your horn at the driver who cut you off, you flash a bright smile, wave, and sing a hymn of praise to God? By employing God's weapons of joy and praise, you ruin Satan's attempt to get you to respond in an ungodly way. In other words, you leave the situation in the spirit realm, where God reigns supreme and the enemy has no power. It is impossible for flesh to win over the spirit when your mind is renewed day by day in the Word of God (Romans 12:1,2; Galatians 5:16). It's only by using spiritual weapons like joy and praise that you gain victory over temptation, sin, and the enemy.

Joy—An Act of the Will

Contrary to popular belief, joy is not just feeling happy all the time or walking around with a smile on your face. Instead, it is an act of the will that has its source in what you know. In other words, it comes by hearing and reading the Word of God. Now, the devil is fully aware that God's Word contains power. In fact, his words are designed to take away your confidence in God's words. Matthew 13:19 tells us that the *"...wicked one...catcheth away..."* that which was sown in your heart. The devil attempts to snatch the Word away as soon as you hear it by quickly contradicting it.

This happened to Adam and Eve in the Garden

of Eden. God had given Adam specific instructions not to eat from the tree of the knowledge of good and evil. But what happened? Almost immediately Satan, through a serpent, contradicted the Word of God. He asked them, *"...Yea, hath God said, Ye shall not eat of every tree of the garden?"* (Genesis 3:1). In essence, Satan planted doubt in their hearts by questioning God's command, and consequently His motives. As a result, Adam and Eve disobeyed God and were punished for it (vv.6-24).

The Fuse to Your Faith

Joy has its source in the Word of God. Think about it. When something becomes real, or rhema to you, don't you get excited? Of course! That's because you have gained understanding of a new concept. You have been set free in that particular area. That's what Jesus meant when he said, *"...ye shall know the truth, and the truth shall make you free"* (John 8:32). It's knowledge—the complete understanding of the Word—that gives freedom and brings a confidence and peace that can only come from the Word you've just received. That's when joy kicks in. Joy is an unwavering belief that God's Word will always come to pass regardless of the circumstances.

This is why it's so important to walk in joy on a daily basis. It gives you the strength to carry on even when your doctor gives you a bad report, when your bills are overdue, or when your electricity gets cut off. It helps you to stand your ground in order to receive the end result of your faith—whatever you're believing God for. If anyone understood this, it was David. He was able to stay encouraged and focused on God in spite of assassination attempts, the kidnapping of his wife, the death of a child, and the insurrection of his son, Absalom. Psalm 16:11 says, *"...in thy presence is fulness of joy...."* God's presence makes joy complete. In other words, joy strengthens and supplies you with heavenly provision. Nehemiah echoed this principle. He said, *"...the joy of the Lord is your strength"* (Nehemiah 8:10). That's why the devil is out to steal it. Joy not only produces strength, but it also contains everything you need to succeed.

Joy is the fuse to your faith. It ignites something on the inside of you that helps you to overcome every obstacle in your path. That's why every believer should be full of joy. First Peter 1:3-9 tells us that when our joy remains in the midst of tribulation we will receive *"...the end of [our] faith..."* (v. 9). That's why James told us to count it all joy whenever we face trials of any kind (James 1:1-3). Joy retrieves stolen property from the enemy's camp. How? Because it is based on the Word of God, it strengthens your confessions, thereby causing God to move quickly on your behalf.

Defend Your Joy

It's important that you defend your joy at all costs. That means evaluating the relationships you have with the people around you. It's impossible to hang around immature Christians and not become immature yourself. Think about it. If you hang out with people who complain and speak negatively about their situations and circumstances, more than likely you will do the same thing. It may not be evident at first, but after awhile the change will show.

For example, if you are hearing "I'll never get out of debt," "I'll never have enough money to live like I really want," or "I'll never get the raise I need at this job," you'll start agreeing with those negative confessions. The person who lets words like these come out of their mouth will have exactly what they say. Words are powerful, and they dictate our very lives. According to Proverbs 18:21, death and life are in the power of the tongue. To speak this way creates a death cycle not only in your prayer life, but also life in general.

However, if you spend time with people who lift up the Word of God above their circumstances, you will do the same. Paul tells us in 1 Corinthians 15:33 that *"...evil communications corrupt good manners;"* however, he who walks with the wise becomes wise (Proverbs 13:20). You must cut off negative relationships before they eat away at the joy in your life.

Power In Praise

The weapon of praise acts in much the same way as the weapon of joy. Both produce and release strength to overcome and defeat the enemy, and both are an act of the will. Praise involves a fixed heart and mind. It requires you to lay aside your fleshly desires and instead offer thanks to God for Who He is and His ability to work on your behalf. This can be a very difficult thing to do, especially when your circumstances look grim. But that's the key to praise. When you lift up God's name, you rise above the circumstances in your life.

So what does it mean to praise? Does it mean to jump around? Shout? Clap hands? Yes, yes, and yes again. Praise is a way of expressing our gratitude to God and also a way of expressing our expectation of what He will do and what He has already done for us. To *praise* means "to commend, applaud, or express approval, and admiration of." It also means to "magnify, glorify, and extol in words or song." Praise paves the way for God to move. That's why most churches begin their services with praise and worship. It encourages the congregation to focus on God and also prepares their hearts to receive new revelation from His Word. Without it, more than likely our services would be unfocused and the people unprepared to hear from God.

Praise is characterized by celebration. In other words, the same enthusiasm that people have when attending a football game is the same type of expressiveness we should have when praising God in church or at home. Praise can take on many different forms: clapping and shouting (Psalm 47:1), standing up as a sign of reverence (Psalm 135:1-3), singing (Acts 16:25), and dancing (Psalm 150:4). Each of these forms may seem strange or irreverent to those who come from a more conservative background; however, it's important to remember that the traditions of men must not be allowed to rule in place of the Word of God. In fact, tradition is what caused David's wife, Michal, to despise him when he stripped off his armor and danced before the Lord (2 Samuel 6:16).

Tradition can prevent you from experiencing the

fullness of joy that comes through praise. And while it's true that the Word of God should shape expressions of your praise, the opinions of those around you should not limit them. Besides that, when you praise God before you see the manifestation of your prayers, it confuses the devil to no end. When the enemy realizes that he can no longer steal your joy, he will have no choice but to move on!

So as you go through the process of eliminating debt from your life once and for all, praise God for every victory. Don't wait until all your debt is gone before you begin thanking Him for Who He is and what He has done for you. Instead, praise Him and Him only for every increase, both small and great.

Let me tell you something. God loves it when you give Him praise. Psalm 35:27 says He delights in the prosperity of His servants. Every dollar that is cancelled on your behalf takes you one step closer to fulfilling the covenant God made with Abraham in Deuteronomy 8:18, which says *"...it is he that giveth thee power to get wealth, that he may establish his covenant...."* As the seed of Abraham and a joint heir with Christ, this is God's promise to you (Romans 8:17). Don't become arrogant and say in your heart that it was your power and might that made you rich (Deuteronomy 8:17). Continue to pray, praise and remain humble before God so that He can continue to bless and exalt you.

Always a Reason to Praise

Whether you realize it or not, there is always a reason to praise God. Think about it. How much has He done for you in the past several years? Weeks? Days? Praise is not based on emotions, but rather on a quality decision to lift God above your circumstances. You must not allow your emotions to dictate whether or not you will praise. Why? That hinders God from effectively working on your behalf. The prophet Habakkuk understood this principle. After losing everything he owned, he sang a hymn of praise to God and outlined his commitment to the Lord in spite of everything that had happened or could ever happen to him.

> Habakkuk 3:17-19
>
> *Although the fig tree shall not blossom, neither shall fruit be in the vines; the labour of the olive shall fail, and the fields shall yield no meat; the flock shall be cut off from the fold, and there shall be no herd in the stalls: Yet I will rejoice in the Lord, I will joy in the God of my salvation. The Lord God is my strength, and he will make my feet like hinds' feet, and he will make me to walk upon mine high places....*

Praise does not benefit God as much as it benefits us. Of course he enjoys it. He is worthy of honor and praise. However, the primary function of praise is to take our minds off of our problems and focus them on the solution—God Almighty. Paul and Silas put this to practice after they had been severely beaten and then wrongfully imprisoned by the Roman government for preaching the gospel of Christ. Now, something like that could really discourage a person from preaching the gospel. But not these two men! Instead of whining and complaining about their situation, Paul and Silas simply began to lift up the name of God. Acts 16:25,26 tells us, *"...at midnight Paul and Silas prayed, and sang praises unto God: and the prisoners heard them. And suddenly there was a great earthquake, so that the foundations of the prison were shaken: and immediately all the doors were opened, and every one's bands were loosed."* Their spontaneous praise in the midst of tribulation unleashed the power of God to move on their behalf, setting them and everyone else with them free. As a result of this supernatural event, the jailer and his entire household got saved.

Become a Weapons Expert

It's important to understand that joy and praise do not come without effort on your part. They are weapons that must be picked up and used on a daily basis. And like any weapon, they must be used correctly before they have any real effect on the enemy. The only way to do this is to practice using them every day. This means continually getting the Word of God into your ears, before your eyes, and in your heart. Hebrews 5:14 tells us that the only way to become an expert in the things of God is through the constant use of His Word. Practice makes perfect.

✗   ✗   ✗   ✗

Without joy and praise, we hinder God's ability to work on our behalf to overcome the enemy. The power and provision we need to overcome obstacles and live successfully is found in these two "invisible" weapons. Purpose in your heart to stop giving in to demonic attack and intimidation. Maintain high levels of joy and praise daily, and see the deliverance of the Lord!

8
The Principle Thing

Chapter 8

The Principle Thing

"Get wisdom, get understanding: forget it not...Wisdom is the principal thing; therefore get wisdom: and with all thy getting get understanding" (Proverbs 4:5,7).

When I was a child, my mother used to make apple pies from scratch. Before she began, she gathered all of the ingredients together: salt, sugar, water, apples, cinnamon, and flour. She did exactly what the recipe instructed her to do. As a result, her pies always came out perfectly. If she had not followed the recipe, and instead tried to substitute the apples with oranges, the pies would have been disasters. She knew the only way to produce delicious, edible treats was to use the right ingredients and follow the instructions.

Getting out of debt is similar to baking an apple pie. You must first have the recipe in front of you—the Word of God—in order for you to know what is needed and how to put it all together to get the results you desire. And just as an apple is the main ingredient in an apple pie, wisdom is the key ingredient to your debt cancellation. In fact, wisdom unlocks the door to anything we need in life. It is the answer to every problem, question, situation, and circumstance we encounter. By obtaining it, we can overcome any obstacle in our path and receive God's abundance.

A Facet of the Anointing

Wisdom is one of the most important character-istics of the Holy Spirit mentioned in Isaiah 11:2. *"And the spirit of the Lord shall rest upon him, the spirit of wisdom and understanding, the spirit of counsel and might, the spirit of knowledge and of the fear of the Lord."* In other words, wisdom is part of the burden-removing, yoke-destroying power of God—the same power that operated through Jesus and that is in us today. It gives direction and provides guidance. And by operating in this powerful anointing, you can experience *sweatless*, or "effortless" debt cancellation. You will no longer try to work out your debt deliverance in your own strength and with your own limited knowledge. Instead, God will work it out for you in His perfect strength.

Now before you can obtain wisdom, you must have a good understanding of what it really is. Contrary to what you may think, wisdom is not knowledge. Instead, it is the force that illuminates knowledge or gives knowledge direction. For example, you can study the Pythagorean Theorem until you're blue in the face, but unless you know how to use it in your everyday living, it doesn't do you any good.

Jesus understood this principle. Take a look at what happened when He fed the 5,000.

Mark 6:35-43

And when the day was now far spent, his disciples came unto him, and said, This is a desert place, and now the time is far passed: Send them away, that they may go into the country round about, and into the villages, and buy themselves bread: for they have nothing to eat. He answered and said unto them, Give ye them to eat. And they say unto him, Shall we go and buy two hundredpennyworth of bread, and give them to eat? He saith unto them, How many loaves have ye? go and see. And when they knew, they say, Five, and two fishes. And he commanded them to make all sit down by companies upon the green grass. And they sat down in ranks, by hundreds, and by fifties. And when he had taken the five loaves and the two fishes, he looked up to heaven, and blessed, and brake the loaves, and gave them to his disciples to set before them; and the two fishes divided he among them all. And they all did eat, and were filled. And they took up twelve baskets full of the fragments, and of the fishes.

It's worth noting that the disciples had enough common sense to realize they did not have enough food to feed everyone standing on the shore that day. However, this basic knowledge of the situation was not enough to solve the problem. That's when the anointing of wisdom kicked in. Instead of panicking or whining over the situation, Jesus took the two-piece fish dinner, blessed it, and then passed it around. As a result, over 5,000 people were fed, and there were enough leftovers to fill 12 baskets!

Now, take a moment to imagine what the disciples must have thought when Jesus told them to command the people to sit down. There was no way in the world to get enough food to feed the crowd, let alone just their little group. Common sense was telling them to send the people away. However, contrary to what "common sense" may have been telling Him, Jesus did something out of the ordinary—He blessed the food. This happened because Jesus knew that the wisdom of God would seem foolish to those who are of the world (1 Corinthians 1:25). There was no sense in trying to explain it to His disciples just yet; instead, He showed them how to operate in wisdom by praying, stepping out in faith and believing that God would meet the needs of the people. And that's exactly what He did, glory to God!

Part of the Initial Deposit

Wisdom is not some unattainable force floating around in the atmosphere. It is an anointing—a part of the Holy Spirit—that lives on the inside of us. Ephesians 1:3 tells us that we have been given every spiritual blessing in Christ. When you became born-again, the Holy Spirit took up permanent residence inside of you (vv. 13,14). At that moment, you received everything that is a part of Him—every characteristic, anointing and facet of His personality. He is the "initial deposit" that guarantees your inheritance of salvation, or soteria—protection, safety, soundness, provision, and prosperity.

It's important to understand that just because we have this initial deposit of the Holy Spirit we should not let His anointing stagnate in our lives. On the contrary, we must learn how to tap into it, and then do our best to increase that anointing. We do this through careful, diligent study of the Word of God, which is wisdom itself. In fact, you can substitute the phrase "Word of God," for the term wisdom anywhere in the Bible.

To get wisdom, you must get an understanding of the Word. Without understanding, the Word will not become rhema, or real, to you. As a result, you will be unable to apply the Word to your daily living, making it difficult, if not impossible, for the promises of God to come to pass in your life. This is why I preach with simplicity and understanding. It does my congregation no good to sit and listen to a great-sounding sermon every Sunday and get nothing out of it to change their lives. They'll never mature spiritually if all I ever do is teach above their heads. They must fully understand the Word to get anything out of it.

Wisdom From the Word

Proverbs 4:5 commands us to *"Get wisdom..."* because it's the principle, or most important thing (v. 7). Without it, you cannot obtain the blessings of God.

Wisdom—the Word of God—shows you exactly what you need to do to receive the manifestation of those blessings. But it does more than that—it promotes, protects, and gives life. It leads you down the path God has predestined you to take—one without distractions or regrets. By aligning yourself with the Word of God, you prepare the way for wisdom to operate through and for you. The Bible assures us that when this happens, no one will be able to resist the words that come out of our mouths (Luke 21:15). When you speak and live by the Word of God, you speak and live by wisdom.

Solomon had first-hand knowledge of this principle. First Kings 3:3-9 tells us that when he was crowned king after the death of his father, David, he prayed not for wealth and favor but for wisdom and a *discerning,* or "hearing" heart. He knew there was no way to successfully govern God's people without wisdom. As a result, his simple request pleased God so much that He gave Solomon more than what he asked for. Not only was Solomon blessed with wisdom, but also wealth beyond measure. *"Behold...*

*I have given thee a wise and an understanding heart;
so that there was none like thee before thee, neither
after thee shall any arise like unto thee. And I have also
given thee...riches, and honour: so that there shall not
be any among the kings like unto thee all thy days"* (1
Kings 3:12,13).

Solomon's wealth and wisdom did not come out
of the blue. He sowed for it. In fact, the Bible tells us
he gave 1,000 burnt offerings and received a hundred
times more than what he asked for (1 Kings 3:4, 10-13;
1 Kings 10:23). That in itself was a form of wisdom in
operation. Solomon was fully aware that he needed
favor with God, and that the way to get it was to
humble himself before the Lord prior to making his
request known. He simply followed the example of his
father, David, who said, "...neither will I offer burnt
offerings unto the Lord my God of that which doth cost
me nothing" (2 Samuel 24:24). As a result of his
integrity and desire to please God, Solomon received
the answer to his request that very night in a dream
(1 Kings 3:5).

A Valuable Asset

Child of God, it's not fair to expect God to give you something for nothing. That violates the Kingdom of God principle of seedtime and harvest found in Galatians 6:7. You must sow in order to reap. Solomon's offering was so extravagant that it got God's attention (2 Chronicles 1:3-12). But more importantly, it was Solomon's attitude—his willingness to do whatever it took to obtain the wisdom of God— that gave him immediate results.

The wisdom of God must be obtained at all costs. I say this because you never know when you're going to need it. You can't wait until the last minute to ask for or operate in the anointing of wisdom. For example, several years ago, one of my employees stole over $10,000 from the ministry. To be perfectly honest, for a moment there I wanted to jump all over him once I found out about the situation. What bothered me the most is not how much he stole, or even who it was that stole the money. The problem was that the television bill was due in a few days, and because of what he had done, it looked as if we would not be able to meet the financial obligation. Immediately my mind began to think of ways to get the money back. But God had another plan in mind.

After I finally sought God for direction, He spoke to my heart and told me exactly what I needed to do. He took me to several scriptures (Matthew 6:12; Luke 6:37) to prepare my heart for what He wanted me to do. The instruction was simple: forgive the man of the offense; call the television stations to explain the situation, and ask for an extension. To be honest, that was hard on my flesh. I wanted to make that man return what he had stolen—with interest! Instead I chose the better way and yielded myself to the wisdom of God, regardless of how irrational His instruction seemed at the time. As a result of my obedience and willingness to forgive, every station manager I called that day waived the television bill for that month. In the end, I reaped more than I lost. Glory to God! He had instructed me in what I needed to do and provided a way out of the situation.

Don't Reject Wisdom's Instruction

Don't be surprised at some of the things God will instruct you to do. He may tell you to call someone who owes you money and forgive their debt. In other words, He may tell you to just forget about it. Well, that's seed sown. You'll no doubt get more from that harvest than you would if the person just gave you the money. Learn to rely on God's wisdom. Remember, His way is tried and perfect (Psalm 18:30).

What would have happened if I had rejected the wisdom of God concerning the $10,000 that was stolen? More than likely I would have been kicked off the air. You see, I didn't wait until the last minute to cultivate a relationship with God or His Word. The ability to hear from God and operate in His wisdom only comes by spending time with Him on a daily basis. That is how Jesus Himself was able to operate in wisdom. If you study Scripture carefully, you'll discover that Jesus' life was a pattern: prayer, miracles, prayer, miracles, prayer, miracles. He did nothing without first seeking direction from God. As a result, every word He spoke was wisdom (Matthew 13:54).

In addition to giving direction to knowledge, wisdom also produces knowledge that has not been previously obtained through study. For example, there is a small percentage of college graduates who have been unable to succeed in the work force simply because they don't know how to use the information they have gathered in school. However, there are high school dropouts who have become the CEOs of major corporations because they have learned the secret of success—wisdom. Wisdom gave them an idea to develop an internet-based company. And wisdom told them how to market their products. In the natural, they did not have the reservoir of knowledge needed to make their businesses profitable. But, they didn't let that stop them. They just tapped into wisdom.

Just as He has done for others, God has a plan or idea that could make you a millionaire overnight. And although God has a million ways to get you out of debt, you only need one. Tap into His wisdom to find out what He has in store for you.

Wisdom at Work

How do you know when wisdom is at work in your life? It can be seen. That's how the Queen of Sheba came to know about Solomon. She had heard about his wealth and wisdom and came to see it for herself. What she saw made her lose her spirit, or faint (1 Kings 10:4-7).

Wealth is a side effect of wisdom, just as an aroma is a side effect of cooking. It can't help but to bring forth riches (Psalm 104:24), find out witty inventions (Proverbs 8:12), and cause everything you have to double up (Job 11:6). With benefits like these, why in the world would anyone want to turn away from it? That's ridiculous. That's like a person who falls into a pit and refuses to climb the ladder someone has provided for an escape! It just doesn't make sense to refuse a God-given method for success.

Tap Into Wisdom

Your debt cancellation will not come from working overtime, having two or three jobs, or hoarding your money. Neither will it come from an inconsistent walk with Christ. Debt deliverance comes by applying the principles of wisdom found in the Word of God. You must make a quality decision to turn away from the world's system and turn toward God's method of sweatless, guaranteed success. His plan is that you work smarter, not harder.

It's important to remember that everyone in the Bible who experienced great success, wealth, and results operated in the anointing of wisdom. Bezaleel and Aholiab put together the tent of meeting for the Israelites (Exodus 31:1-6). Joshua led the Israelites into the Promised Land and defeated the enemies of God (Deuteronomy 34:9). And Solomon reigned successfully over the kingdom of Israel (1 Kings 4:29) until he turned away from God's Word—the very thing that protected him from destruction.

✗   ✗   ✗   ✗

Wisdom is the master key to debt cancellation. It illuminates the path to God's abundance but must be sought after more than wealth. If you continually employ wisdom in your life, you will not only *obtain* wealth, but you will also have the ability to *retain* it. It does you no good to get out of debt and then find yourself in the same hole a few weeks or months later. Wisdom is a powerful tool designed to help you live the abundant life Jesus promised in John 10:10. But it's up to you to employ it in your daily living. Make a quality decision now to become all God desires you to be through the anointing of wisdom.

Conclusion

Money With a Mission

Conclusion

Money With a Mission

"The Lord is my strength and song, and he is become my salvation: he is my God, and I will prepare him an habitation; my father's God, and I will exalt him" (Exodus 15:2).

Your money has a mission. That means God already has a purpose for getting you out of debt and putting wealth into your hands. As children of the Most High and the seed of Abraham, we have been called to fulfill the mandate given in Genesis 12:3, to be blessed—empowered to prosper and excel—so that we can be a blessing to others.

Based on Deuteronomy 8:18, God has given us the power to get wealth. But that power is contingent upon one thing: meditating on the Word of God daily. That doesn't mean reading scriptures on debt cancellation or prosperity every once in a while, and then expecting God to do something supernatural on your behalf. That's not how the system works. To *meditate* means "to ponder." In other words, thinking about God's Word so much that your life is changed by it.

You Must Have the Right Motive

Now here is where many Christians miss it. They read the biblical accounts of supernatural debt deliverance, shout "money cometh" three times a day and sow continually, but they have yet to receive the manifestation of what they are believing God for. Why? The attitude of their hearts is in direct conflict with their outward actions. In other words, they have not renewed their minds in this area and have the wrong motives for getting wealth. The wrong motive with the right action is still disobedience, and it doesn't get you anywhere with God.

You must be desperate to get out of debt. Desperate people do desperate things to solve their problems. That's what happened to me. I got to the point where I was so fed up with being in debt, that I was willing to try anything—even God's way—to get out of it. God's way worked! However, it didn't happen overnight. And it certainly didn't happen because I was unfaithful with God's money. On the contrary, I was very careful to obey God in everything I did. And by meditating on what God had to say about wealth completely changed my motives for obtaining it. I wanted wealth just to give it away. Like David, my heart's desire was to build temples for God (1 Chronicles 28:2). But not temples made out of stone; rather, temples made out of flesh and blood (1 Corinthians 3:16).

Change is Necessary

Positioning yourself to receive God's promised abundance is not the easiest thing to do because it involves change—a change of heart, mind, and motives. You must be willing and able to see the bigger picture. In fact, you must be able to see the world through the eyes of a loving, merciful, and compassionate God who desires to meet the needs of His people and bring the lost into the kingdom. Without His heart, your money is worthless.

It's important to understand that God wants you out of debt for a reason—to build up His kingdom by blessing others with your finances. That means we are under an obligation to get out of debt and get out quickly. That doesn't mean debate the issue. Paul made it plain when he said, *"Owe no man any thing, but to love one another...."* (Romans 13:8). Debt cancellation is not an option, but a command from Almighty God. God cannot do all of the things He desires to do through you if you are still mired down with debt. How can you bless others financially if you don't have anything to spare?

A complete renewal of the mind is necessary for debt cancellation. That means leaving behind your old ways of thinking and believing. You must purpose in your heart to get rid of the poverty mentality once and for all—the mentality that says if I give, I will lose everything. That's simply not true! God desires to get wealth into your hands; however, before He can do that, He must know beyond a shadow of a doubt that you trust Him and will do exactly what He tells you to do with the money He gives you. Obedience is the key to opening the doors of abundance.

But wealth transference is only a small part of the big picture. Money is a tool designed to build up the kingdom by meeting the needs of others. When you sow financially into the life of another person, you are making God real to them. This in turn plants the seed of desire within them—a desire to know God more intimately. It's for this reason we have been commanded to *"...Go...into all the world..."*(Mark 16:15). We have been called to pursue the needs of others. In other words, we are a blessing waiting to happen. That's why it's vitally important that we get out of debt—we must be ready at all times to sow where and when God tells us to.

Accept the Mission

It's vitally important that you understand the ultimate goal of financial blessings. When you don't understand the purpose for something, abuse is inevitable. Judge yourself carefully. If you are not ready for the mission, you just aren't ready for God's money. It's that simple. Purpose in your heart to obey God financially. Allow Him to guide your giving and show you the way out of debt. Accept the divine mission for your money, and reap the rewards of endless abundance and victorious living.

Confession

In the name of Jesus, I accept the mission God has placed before me—to receive wealth in order to bless all families of the earth. I am out of debt. My needs are met. I have plenty more to put in store. Money cometh to me, now! And Father, as You equip me, I declare that I will dispense Your prosperity throughout the world

because I am a distribution center. Thank You, Lord, for giving me wealth for someone else's good. In Jesus' name, Amen.

Countdown to
Debt Cancellation

Countdown to Debt Cancellation

Listed below is a simple checklist to follow as you begin your journey toward permanent debt cancellation and prosperous living. Be sure to actively employ each step daily until you see the desired results.

Step 1: Develop a clear understanding that God desires for you to live an abundant life here on earth (John 10:10), and then make a quality decision to get out and stay out of debt.

Step 2: Build your faith and confidence in God by diligently studying what His Word has to say concerning debt cancellation.

Step 3: Gather all your bills together in one place. On a sheet of paper write your declaration of independence from debt and place it with your bills.

Step 4: Recite aloud how much you owe to whom as well as your scriptures on debt cancellation. Do this several times daily until you see results.

Step 5: Bind the strongman (debt) and loose the angels of God to bring forth your harvest.

Step 6: Tithe into a Word-based church and obey God in your giving. Be sure to give cheerfully!

Step 7: Sow into the life of an anointed man or woman of God. Become a partner with the anointing that is on their lives.

Step 8: Maintain high levels of joy, prayer and praise. Begin thanking God now for the manifestation of debt release, and remember to give Him the glory for every victory, no matter how small.

Step 9: Guard you heart and refuse the temptation to speak negatively against your financial situation.

Step 10: Don't reject God's instruction, no matter how strange it may seem. Obedience brings provision. Remember, one Word from God is all it takes to change your life forever!

Step 11: Always keep the mission for wealth at the forefront of your thinking (Genesis 12:3)!

Study Questions

Chapter 1

A New Way of Life

1. There are two financial systems at work in the earth today. What are they?

2. What is the Kingdom of God system? How does it work?

3. List three of the world's methods for debt cancellation.

4. Explain the difference between God's method of debt cancellation and the world's.

5. What is the principle found in Galatians 6:7? Why is it important to remember?

6. Your job should be an avenue for obtaining what?

7. How can a renewed mind help you get out of debt?

8. What are five things you should remember when you sow a seed?

Chapter 2

Tuning In to God's Frequency

1. Why is the ability to hear God clearly one of the most important things a Christian should learn?

2. Write down one scripture that will help to support your decision to hear God's voice.

3. How can you hear from God?

4. List two reasons why many Christians have difficulty hearing from God.

5. What are the benefits of communing with God?

6. Do you think you have an undeveloped spirit? Why or why not?

7. How does your spirit grow?

8. Explain the importance of forgiveness.

9. List five things you must do in order to position yourself to hear God's voice.

10. What four things will God's instructions always do?

Chapter 3

The Practical Side to Debt Cancellation

1. What are the two most common reasons people give for staying in debt?

2. What New Testament scripture promotes prosperity?

3. List two places in the Bible where God promises to prosper His children.

4. As the seed of Abraham what are we entitled to? What is the purpose for it?

5. What is the purpose for keeping your bills in order?

6. What is a "poverty mentality"? How can it hinder you from receiving debt cancellation?

7. What is the purpose for writing down how much you owe to whom and reciting it aloud daily?

8. Proverbs 18:21 tells us that the tongue contains the power of life and death. Do you agree with this statement? Why or why not?

9. What opens the windows of heaven over your life and connects you to the covenant promises of God? What scripture is this based on?

10. What is "tithing the tithe"?

Chapter 4

The Building Blocks of Debt Cancellation

1. Why is your mouth the most powerful tool for debt cancellation?

2. What is a title deed? Why is it important to have one?

3. List three title deeds from the Word of God concerning your debt release.

4. Why is it vital that you deposit the Word of God in your heart daily?

5. What are some of the weapons Satan uses to weaken your faith?

6. Why is it important to write down your vision?

7. What is the formula for getting things manifested in the physical realm?

8. Why is patience important?

9. Why is the Word of God the basic building block for everything in life?

Chapter 5

A Partner With the Anointing

1. What happens when you decide to partner with the anointing?

2. List the benefits of partnering with the anointing.

3. How do you partner with the anointing?

4. How can you tell whether or not a minister/ministry is anointed?

5. Why does partnership involve financial giving?

6. List two biblical examples in which a man of God was the central figure for a financial miracle in the lives of those who sowed into his life.

7. Why does the Word describe a double-minded man as unstable?

Chapter 6

Entertaining Angels

1. What is the main duty of angels?

2. What does the Greek word *soteria* mean?

3. How often can you call on God for soteria after you become born again? Why?

4. List five examples from the Word of God where angels ministered to God's people.

5. Why are angels so important to your debt deliverance?

6. What causes angels to move on your behalf?

Chapter 7

Weapons of Warfare

1. According to 1 Peter 5:8, the devil does what?

2. Satan can also be called "the Great Pretender." What are the two weapons he uses against Christians?

3. How do joy and praise form a protective barrier against demonic attack?

4. Write down your definition of joy. Does it differ from God's? If so, how?

5. How does joy ignite your faith?

6. How does praise work?

7. List four ways in which praise can be characterized.

8. Why is it important to walk in an attitude of joy and praise daily?

Chapter 8

The Principle Thing

1. What does wisdom provide?

2. How does the anointing of wisdom help you to experience sweatless debt cancellation?

3. What is the key to tapping into the wisdom of God?

4. Does wisdom promote, protect and give life? How?

5. What did Solomon do before petitioning God? Did it work?

6. What did Solomon pray for in 1 Kings 3:3-9 that brought him such great wealth?

7. How do you develop the ability to hear from God and operate in His wisdom?

8. How do you know when wisdom is at work in your life?

Five Steps to Complete Salvation

1. Recognize and admit that you are a sinner (Psalm 51:5).

2. Repent of your sins (1 John 1:9).

3. Confess Jesus Christ as Lord and Savior (Romans 10:9,10).

    Father, in the name of Jesus, I recognize and admit that I am a sinner. I repent of my sin and I make a 180° turn away from sin to You by changing my heart, mind and direction. I confess with my mouth that Jesus is Lord, and I believe in my heart that You raised Him from the dead. I invite You to come into my life, Lord Jesus, and I thank You that I am saved. Amen.

4. Receive baptism by water (Matthew 3:6) and the baptism of the Holy Spirit with the evidence of speaking in tongues (Acts 2:3,4, 38; Acts 8:14-17).

5. Pray, read, and obey the Word of God daily (1 John 5:3).

Seven Steps to Receiving the Baptism of the Holy Spirit

1. The Holy Spirit is a gift that was given on the day of Pentecost (Acts 2:38).

2. Salvation is the only qualification necessary for receiving the Holy Spirit (Acts 2:38).

3. The laying on of hands is scriptural (Acts 8:17).

4. You can expect to speak in tongues when hands are laid on you (Acts 19:6).

5. Disregard any fears or false teachings about receiving a counterfeit (Luke 11:11-13).

6. Open your mouth as an act of faith (Ephesians 5:18,19).

7. Receive the gift of speaking in tongues in an atmosphere of peace (1 Corinthians 14:33).

If You Would Like:

• To order books and tapes by Dr. Creflo A. Dollar Jr.

• To become a partner or supporter of Creflo Dollar Ministries

• To obtain a free copy of the Changing Your World Magazine

• To become an e-mail subscriber and receive the latest information concerning ministry events, new releases and special offers

Call us:
United States and Canada................1-888-252-7788
United Kingdom...................... 011-44-121-326-9889
Australia.. 61-7-5528-1144
South Africa.................................... 27-11-792-5562

or
Visit our Web site: www.worldchangers.org